The
FLY TYER'S
PRIMER

BOOKS BY RICHARD W. TALLEUR

FLY FISHING FOR TROUT: *A Guide for Adult Beginners*
MASTERING THE ART OF FLY TYING
THE FLY TYER'S PRIMER

The
FLY TYER'S
PRIMER

Richard W. Talleur

NICK LYONS BOOKS

WINCHESTER PRESS

An Imprint of New Century Publishers, Inc.

Produced by
NICK LYONS BOOKS
31 West 21 Street
New York, NY 10010

Published and distributed by
WINCHESTER PRESS
New Century Publishers, Inc.
220 Old New Brunswick Road
Piscataway, NJ 08854

Printed in the United States of America

10 9 8 7 6 5 4 3 2 1

Talleur, Richard W.
    The fly-tyer's primer.

    "Nick Lyons books."
    1. Fly tying.   I. Title.
SH451.T286   1986   688.7′9   86-2774
ISBN 0–8329–0423–6

CONTENTS

All line drawings by
ERNEST LUSSIER

Color and black-and-white photographs by
DEE WEIDIG

DICK TALLEUR—*drawn by Ernest Lussier*

PROLOGUE

In 1979, Stackpole Books (Harrisburg, Pennsylvania) published my book *Mastering the Art of Fly-Tying*. Response to that work has been both gratifying and exciting.

Although *Mastering the Art of Fly-Tying* was written for the intermediate-level tyer, who had already achieved a modicum of skill, it has also been pressed into service as a beginner's instruction manual. And while some of the material is within the scope of a novice who is also receiving other instruction in fundamental fly-tying techniques, many basics were omitted. I felt at the time that trying to create a combined beginner's/intermediate book was a bit ambitious, and I think I was right.

Recent experiences in teaching fly-tying seminars indicate that a need exists for a true beginner's text—a primer, if you will. I am constantly encountering people who want to get started in tying and need assistance. This book is for them.

A few words of explanation are necessary so that the reader will not be confused by some slight disparities between the text and the accompanying photographs. In some cases, I use materials and hand positions that vary from the narrative for purposes of contrast and explicitness. For example, in the chapter Thread Management, I use heavy thread and highly visible materials so that the reader can see clearly what is going on. In certain pattern lessons, I vary some of the components a bit to enhance the contrast. The color pictures are true to shade, so please use them as a guide—and I do mean guide. You will probably want to adapt the shadings to your own preferences and to those of the fish in the waters you frequent.

Also, a bit of clarification regarding terminology is in order. Fly-tying has its own language. You will learn that a grizzly isn't always a bear, a badger an animal, or a cree a Native American. There is some ambiguity in fly-tying parlance. Some terms are used more or less interchangeably; for example, *barbules and fibres, quill and stem, wraps and turns and winds*. *Tying-in* usually refers to affixing a piece of material that will be used in a subsequent operation, whereas *tying on* generally means the component is simply tied in place—but this distinction is not cast in concrete. *Hackle* and *dubbing* refer to materials and also operations—for example to hackle a fly or to dub the body. Having been warned, I don't think the reader will have any difficulty understanding the application of such terms throughout the book.

The techniques and methods set forth in the *Primer* have evolved over nearly a quarter-century of teaching people to tie. Apparently, these methods work well, and I am very pleased with the accomplishments of my numerous pupils. However, this does not mean that my methods are the only ones, or that you must forever slavishly adhere to them. As you develop expertise, you will tend to adapt your fly-tying techniques to suit your particular style—which is as it should be.

When a golf professional teaches the classic grip, stance, and swing to beginning students, they eventually incorporate the basic principles into a game which reflects their own particular bodily articulation. I'm sure Miller Barber's old teaching pro winces as he watches that Sunday-golfer swing on national television—but who can fault success? And so it is with fly-tying. Once you have achieved competence, the wraps are off. Innovate to your heart's content. Maybe you will write the next book and I'll be a customer.

I want to acknowledge the contributions of several individuals whose talents have enhanced this book greatly. My thanks to Bill Hunter of Hunter's Angling Supplies in New Boston, New Hampshire, for his diligent salmon-fly-tying instruction, which really tightened up my techniques, and also for circumspect and relevant observations on materials, tools, etc. Also a large helping of gratitude goes to Ernie Lussier for his world-class art work, his encouragement, and his friendship.

I also want to thank Angling Products, Inc. of Upper Saddle River, New Jersey, makers of the HMH Standard and API Spartan fly-tying vises. API was considerate enough to interrupt a busy schedule to turn out a special nonglare head for my vise that was most helpful in the photography used in this book.

And I want to particularly commend Dee Weidig, my photographer. How she squeezed me into a schedule that already included raising three children, managing a household, going to college, and teaching fly-tying at United Fly Tyers, I do not know. I hope it didn't compromise her fishing schedule too severely. Also, my thanks to the Weidig family for cheerful tolerance of my encroachment on their turf.

While confident that *The Fly Tyer's Primer* will be of great assistance to the fledgling tyer, I cannot overstate the value of personal instruction. There's nothing like a hands-on session for correcting the mistakes and easing the anxieties that are common to all beginners. Organizations such as Trout Unlimited and the Federation of Fly Fishers do a fine job in conducting fly-tying classes, as do many individual teachers. I would implore you to avail yourself of such a resource— it makes the process that much easier.

DICK TALLEUR
May 1985

1

PRINCIPLES OF FLY DESIGN

Welcome to the world of fly-tying. Tying flies is a wonderful skill to learn. Catching fish on your own creations will greatly enhance the pleasures of fly-fishing.

A working knowledge of fly design is a prerequisite to effective fishing—and even more so to effective fly-tying. Whether you create your own patterns or simply dress the classics, it is of great value to understand why a particular fly works. You will then be able to visualize how the fly should look, not only to yourself but to the ever-more-sophisticated fish we attempt to deceive.

All flies may be grouped into two major categories:

• Surface/Subsurface—that is, dry fly or wet fly
• Imitator/Attractor—that is, designed to simulate specific items of food, or not

These classifications are applied to individual flies in combination. For example, the well-known Hendrickson dry fly is a surface imitator. The Parmachene Belle, which dates back to the glorious era of wild brook-trout fishing, is a subsurface attractor.

Perhaps the ultimate example of a pure attractor is the fully dressed Atlantic salmon fly. These spectacular patterns are often complex beyond any definable rationale, limited only by the fly-dresser's ability, imagination, and arsenal of materials. They are used on fish that are physiologically unable to eat during the spawning run, so food is no motivator. It is still not clear why a salmon takes a fly, let alone why a particular pattern is preferred at any given time.

The surface/subsurface method of classification is a great deal more precise than the imitator/attractor method: a fly either floats (dry) or it doesn't (wet). True, there are subclassifications. For example, some dry flies are designed to be high-floaters, whereas others are designed to ride low, or flush to the surface. Some wet flies are designed to be bottom-huggers, while others are designed to barely sink into the surface film. Perhaps these should be called "damp flies." In any event, we shall study all types in the chapters ahead.

Much more complexity is involved when the imitator/attractor criteria are applied to a particular fly. For example, the Hendrickson dry fly was designed to simulate a particular mayfly in the sub-adult, or dun stage (*sub-imago* is the proper Latin term), yet with slight variations, it serves as a credible imitator of a number of mayflies. And sometimes it can be fished effectively when no insects are hatching and fish are not rising. At such times, this fly has to be considered an attractor from a functional standpoint.

Certain flies that were designed with a specific insect in mind make great attractors. I can think of no better example than Art Flick's Grey Fox Variant (a variant is a dry fly with oversized hackles and no wings). Art created the Grey Fox Variant in the image of a large mayfly, which was an important species on many Northeastern streams. It is a high-floater, designed for use in the heavier currents in which the natural insect generally emerges. Today, even though the mayfly hatches that this pattern was designed to represent are far less prolific, the variant is still wonderfully effective in the appropriate setting.

Another prime example of the nonspecific but food-suggestive dry fly is the famous Royal Coachman. This is an old pattern that has gained favor throughout the world—and with good reason. While it does not closely resemble any particular natural insect, the Royal Coachman has several attributes that make it effective. It features striking color contrasts, is highly visible, and is generally suggestive of a floating insect. We will learn to dress the hairwing version of the Royal Coachman in one of the pattern lessons.

Subsurface flies are also difficult to classify precisely as imitators or attractors. As a fledgling angler, I learned that the Leadwing Coachman wet fly was quite deadly when worked through the fast riffles and pockets of the streams in my locality, but I didn't know why. Soon I perceived that this pattern was much more effective at those times when a large, slate-wing mayfly appeared. I was learning the rudiments of hatch-matching. Eventually I discovered that a well-tied nymph pattern was even more successful, because it more closely resembled the life stage during which the naturals were most readily available to the trout.

When is a fly not a fly? Strictly speaking, any fly that doesn't imitate, or at least generally suggest, insect life shouldn't really be called a fly. Streamer flies, which comprise a very large and important school of fly design, are dressed to resemble or suggest small fishes that are part of the diet of trout and other game fish. Actually, they are fly-rod lures. As with insect-type flies, some patterns closely resemble a specific species of baitfish, others are wild-looking attractors, and many fall somewhere in between.

I am perfectly happy to continue referring to streamers as flies, even though they don't imitate real ones. I think it would be more confusing at this late date to rename them—everyone seems to know what a streamer fly is.

At this point, let us summarize:

• True *imitators* are flies that are designed—in terms of size, color, texture, silhouette, and, in some cases, behavioral characteristics—to be mistaken by the fish for a specific natural insect or other dietary item.

• True *attractors* are flies that are designed without specific imitation in mind. They depend for effectiveness on such attributes as visibility to the fish and/or the angler, behavior in or on the water, and contrast to what the fish normally sees about him. I have frequently enjoyed success by "unmatching" a hatch when the trout snubbed my precise imitator. The odd fly that contrasts with its natural counterparts in the water sometimes seems to produce by sheer dint of calling attention to itself.

• There is a large group of flies that are more or less suggestive of insects, baitfish, crustaceans, and other trout foods. This group includes many great producers, such as the Adams dry fly and the Hare's Ear wet fly. Let us call them by that name: *suggestors*.

• Because of their design characteristics, true imitators are usually much more effective in hatch-matching situations. By the same token, suggestors and sometimes pure attractors are better suited for probing the water.

• The fish ultimately decide what is an imitator. If a particular trout thinks a red-and-yellow Mickey Finn streamer looks like a minnow and should be devoured, why argue? Effectiveness is what counts—we use what works.

We have examined fly design from the dual standpoints of whether the fly floats or sinks and whether or not it closely resembles a specific food item. Now let's take another approach, examining fly design as it relates to the environment in which it will be used. By environment, I am referring primarily to water type. The longer I fish, the more I realize that this is perhaps even more important than the precise-imitation aspect.

There are fishermen who, for whatever reason, confine their efforts to one type of water or even to one stream. For them, choosing a fly type which works in their preferred water is all they need be concerned with. However, most of us like to travel around and fish rivers with widely diverse water types. For our contingent, having flies that match up optimally with the various water types is of tremendous importance.

If I am probing the pockets of a wild, boulder-strewn freestone river, I will be doing so with some sort of suggestor fly, be it wet, dry, nymph, or streamer. It will be large enough to catch the fish's eye, even at times when the fish may not be particularly attentive. Maybe I will use a Zug Bug or, if I see stonefly cases on the rocks, a Montana nymph.

If I decide to use a streamer, it will be one that relies on action and creating an illusion for its effectiveness—a marabou pattern, perhaps. Or I may choose a Muddler Minnow, probably the most versatile fly of all, because it suggests so many different things that fish feed upon.

When I'm dry fly fishing, I want a pattern that can be seen in rough water, both by me and by the fish. This suggests a fly of medium to large size, of a shade which doesn't blend in with the water so much that it virtually disappears. And it must be an excellent floater. Flies that come readily to mind include the various Wulffs, the Humpys, and the Variants. As to coloration, I will start with something very general and multishaded, such as the Grey Fox Variant. Ambient light and water clarity will figure into this decision too. I will then experiment until the fish let me know what they want.

Let us imagine that I fish around a bend in the river and find the character of the water has suddenly changed. The gradient is not as sharp, and the stream broadens and slows into more moderate currents. The water is shallower, the current less broken.

Suddenly, my large Variant looks like an albatross on the water—in fact, it may be an albatross around my neck. I clip it off, reduce my leader-tippet diameter by two-thousandths of an inch, and tie on a smaller fly with a cleaner silhouette—a size 14 Adams, perhaps. All of this, of course, assumes no hatching activity or rising trout—I'm still prospecting.

Around the next bend, the stream flattens out into a slow, quiet pool, the surface like glass. Unless I could see that fish were feeding, either on or beneath the surface, I probably wouldn't fish this pool, but I do make exceptions. In such a case, I wouldn't fish dry. I would select a small wet fly or nymph, sparsely hackled, and with a somewhat fuzzy body of translucent material.

Consideration should be given to water type when matching a hatch as well as when prospecting. For example, I will select a different design of Hendrickson dry fly when the naturals are bouncing along a riffle than when they are floating sedately on a smooth pool. I tie conventional Hendricksons and Red Quills for the rougher stretches and sparsely-dressed parachutes or thorax-type flies for the calmer pools.

There is a great deal more to fly design, and this chapter could almost become a book, in and of itself. In the chapter on fly-tying materials, and in the pattern lessons, we will examine the subject further, as it relates to the properties of various materials and the dressing of specific flies.

For now, let's summarize by reiterating that fly design is very much a function of water type and environmental setting, the major considerations being:

• Roughness of surface
• Speed of current
• Depth of water
• Clarity or turbidity of water
• Relative cloudiness or sunshine
• Overall ambient light
• Amount of wind

Consideration of the conditions in which I expect my flies to be used has improved both my tying and my angling success, and it is my pleasure to share these experiences with you.

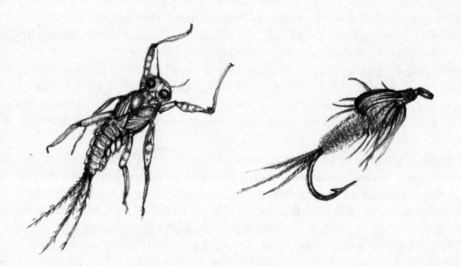

2

THE BASIC TOOL SET

Tools and instruments for fly-tying fall into three main categories: must-have; extremely helpful, almost must-have; and, nice-to-have, but can live without.

Here, we will address only categories one and two. First, the must-haves:

- Fly-tying vise
- Fine-work scissors
- Coarse-work scissors
- Hackle pliers
- Dubbing needle
- Bobbin

THE VISE

The function of a fly-tying vise is to hold the hook perfectly still while the tyer executes the required operations. *Perfectly still* means just that—nothing less is acceptable. Can you imagine a golfer trying to hit a ball which wobbles around on the tee, especially a beginning player? My first vise was a very poor one, so I can relate to the difficulty of learning how to tie on an inadequate tool.

Today, there are many good-quality vises on the market in a wide range of prices, based not only on quality but also on versatility. For example, some vises have several sets of interchangeable jaws that provide optimal hold for the size of hook being used. Some have an angle adjustment feature. Some allow 360-degree rotation of the hook. All of these features have value, but they are not essential to the beginner.

Most vises are of the draw-collet type. This simply means that a lever is employed to draw the jaws rearward into a metal tube, or collet, which causes the jaws to close onto the hook.

A typical vise is designed to optimally handle hooks from size 2 to 20, this being a function of jaw design, adjustment capability, and quality of metal. A few are even more versatile. I have an HMH Spartan, manufactured by Angling Products, Inc. of Upper Saddle River, New Jersey, which accomodates hooks from size 2/0 to 28, given strict attention to proper adjustment.

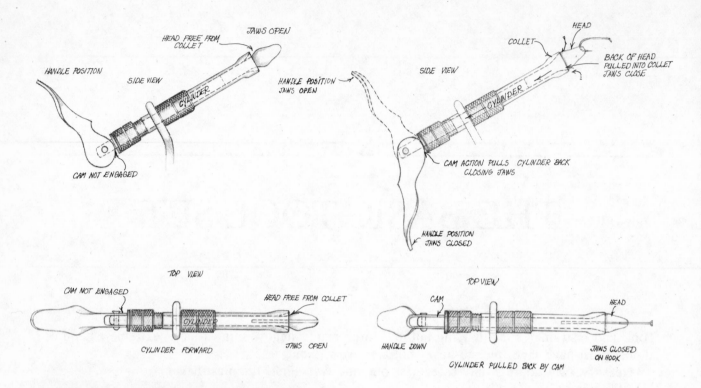

Two vises, showing C-clamp and pedestal base mounts.

Most vises utilize a C-clamp mounting mechanism. Some offer the alternative of a heavily weighted base which simply sits on the tying table. A few feature interchangeable base and C-clamp, as an added-cost option. Each mounting device has its advantages:

C-Clamp
• Vise height can be adjusted
• Light, easy to transport
• Lower cost

Pedestal Base
• Mounts on any flat surface, regardless of thickness
• Can be moved anywhere on tying surface, to optimize light, or whatever
• No chance of damaging a valuable desk or table by inadvertently over-tightening a clamp

Choice of mount is up to the individual. Personally, I favor a C-clamp, because I do a lot of traveling by air and want to minimize weight. However, the potential problem with this is that the clamp must be wider than the thickness of whatever tying surface is encountered. Some of today's better-quality vises have extra-wide clamps—for example, the HMH measures 2½ inches (64 mm), large enough for most desks and tables.

It is important to adjust the jaw setting of the vise for the size—that is, the wire diameter—of hook being used. Too large a gap results in poor gripping, causing the hook to slip. Too small a gap causes the jaw-closing mechanism to engage too early. This is dangerous to the health of the vise, as it may result in a pair of damaged jaws. *Never* force a hook into the jaws of a vise, and *never* apply extreme pressure to the lever in an effort to force the jaws to grip a hook. The typical vise is in proper adjustment when the hook is held immobile with the lever in approximately a six-o'clock position.

How much should a beginner spend on a vise? I would say that if the particular individual is sure he or she wants to stick with it and become a "serious" tyer, a top-quality vise is an excellent investment. It is a life-time tool, or virtually so, and when purchase price is spread over time, true value is realized.

You might think in terms of the type and variety of flies you eventually want to tie. If your objective is to learn to dress basic, average-sized flies, and nothing more, then a moderately priced, unsophisticated vise will serve you well. But if you envision becoming a diversified tyer, it might be wise to invest in a superior-quality vise, such as the HMH Spartan or even the HMH Standard. These vises offer the interchangeable jaws, angle adjustment, and rotation features facilitate working on any type of fly and any hook size. The quality of design, workmanship, and materials is excellent, and the product carries a lifetime guarantee, barring abuse.

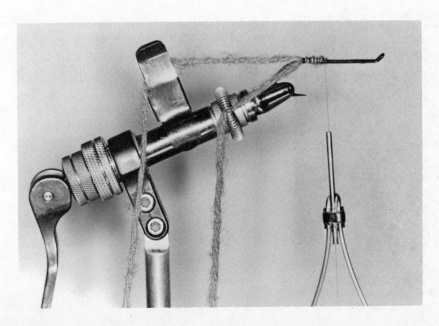

Two different types of materials clips, which attach to the vise and hold material out of the way.

SCISSORS

Two pair of scissors belong on the must-have list. I suppose that if a person wants to tie delicate dry and wet flies, and nothing more, a fine-tipped pair might suffice. However, it is the rare tyer who doesn't also want to dress bucktail streamers, hairwing dry flies, Muddler Minnows, and other styles of flies call for coarser materials. Using one's fine-work scissors for rougher tasks is a serious mistake.

It's advisable to examine scissors before purchasing, especially the fine-work type. Here are the most important criteria:

- Sharpness and fineness of tips and blades
- Evenness or precision of tips and blades
- Hardness of metal
- Tightenable axis screw
- Finger-loop size
- Adequate length
- Good shearing action

Look closely at the blades from both the flat and edged vectors. The blades should not be overly thick or bulky, and the tips should come to a very sharp point and meet perfectly. If one tip is even slightly longer than the other, difficulty will be encountered during delicate operations.

Hardness of metal is somewhat difficult to assess—one almost has to go by the manufacturer's specifications. For example, we know that blades with tungsten-carbide inserts are incredibly hard—so hard that they must be sharpened by a professional. Surgical scissors made of hardened stainless steel are also quite suitable for demanding fly-tying tasks.

Some scissors use a rivet rather than a screw at the point of axis. This is undesirable, because there is no way to tighten up the scissors after they loosen, which they inevitably will. This also relates to good shearing action. In order for blades to shear properly, the point of axis must be tight.

Most of today's fly-tying scissors are adequate in terms of length and finger-loop size. This was not always true years ago, when we often had to buy scissors designed for the hands of a seamstress. Persons with extra-large fingers can now obtain scissors with adjustable finger loops. Or, the loops may be cut with a small file and spread to accomodate the hands of the tyer.

Better fly-tying shops now offer scissors of superior quality. The finest I've yet encountered are

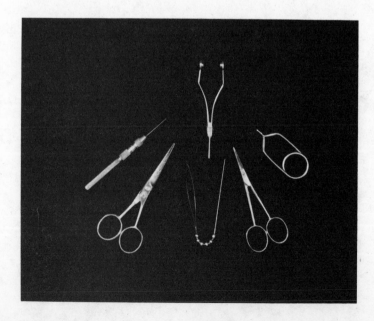

Basic tools, clockwise from top: bobbin, hackle pliers, fine-work scissors, bobbin threader-cleaner, coarse-work scissors, bodkin.

the optical-grade surgical scissors with tungsten-carbide blade inserts sold by Hunter's Fly Shop of New Boston, New Hampshire. The beginner may find these a little high-priced for a first venture and may opt for hardened stainless steel.

For a heavier pair of scissors, I find the small shears currently used by hairdressers to be ideal. They are about 4½ inches (115 mm) in length overall, and have tiny serrations on the blades, which helps when cutting coarse, slippery hairs and furs. Some day, when these scissors must be sharpened, the serrations will disappear, but with average use, it will be years before sharpening is required.

I should mention that scissors well suited for fly-tying may be purchased in speciality stores, such as the Hoffritz chain. During the three-year period I commuted into New York City, I haunted the Grand Central Terminal Hoffritz, often driving the clerks nuts by asking to inspect every pair of a particular model of scissors in the store. I compensated by purchasing a great many pair—I was the supplier for all of my outlander fly-tying friends who never got near a Hoffritz.

HACKLE PLIERS

Hackle pliers are a specialty tool, manufactured expressly for fly-tyers. They are used to grip small, hard-to-handle items, particularly feathers, during certain tying operations.

Typical hackle pliers consist of a spring loop with flattened jaws. On some models, one or both of the jaws are slightly serrated to enhance gripping qualities. This is okay, provided the serrations are not too rough, in which case they can cut or crush delicate feather stems.

We also encounter hackle pliers with a tiny rubber or plastic sleeve covering one of the jaws. I won't argue vehemently against this, but feel it is unnecessary if the tool is properly manufactured and precisely adjusted. Some shops now offer a fine-tuning service whereby the tension and jaw closure of hackle pliers are set at optimum. Not a bad idea.

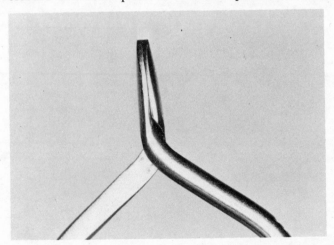

Jaws of hackle pliers, showing perfect occlusion.

DUBBING NEEDLE

Also known as a bodkin, this useful tool is nothing more than a needle mounted in a handle. It has many uses, the most common of which is the application of head cement. Dubbing needles are a low-cost item, available in fly shops. An excellent one can be made by mounting a sturdy needle in a pin vise, which may be obtained in any good hardware store. The advantage here is that the needle can be replaced if it is dulled or broken.

BOBBIN

It could be argued that the bobbin shouldn't be included in a must-have list. True, fly-tying can be done without using a bobbin—in fact I began that way, which I believe entitles me to judge it a must-have. I know the difference.

I do not know of any fly-tyer who has taken up the art during the great renaissance period, which began in the late 1960s, who doesn't use a bobbin. However, some of our great senior tyers still prefer to work the thread by hand. Elsie Darbee, noted Catskill fly-tyer, considered the bobbin a nuisance and, to my knowledge, never owned one. Elsie used a thread clip to maintain tension. She was lightning-quick, and her flies were uniformly perfect. That was fine for her, with those hands. The rest of us need the bobbin.

Overwhelmingly the most popular bobbin in use today is the simple wishbone model. The thread is fed through a tube while tension is maintained by the springy limbs of the bobbin. Quite often, a new bobbin needs to be loosened up, as the tension is too great. This must be done carefully. Don't seize the two limbs and spread them, as though making a wish. Bend out each limb individually, a little at a time. You may want some assistance from a fellow tyer or someone in the shop.

Bobbins come with various tube lengths. I recommend the standard model. One bobbin will suffice, but two make life easier—one for black thread and one for white. The best bobbins are still a low-cost item.

The one problem to watch out for with bobbins is a burr or rough spot on the mouth of the tube. This will become immediately apparent as the thread will inexplicably be frayed or cut. I do not recommend trying to fix this aberration. Return the bobbin to the dealer.

That takes care of the must-haves. Now for the almost-must-haves:
* Bobbin threader-cleaner
* Half-hitch tool
* Hackle guards
* Hair stacker
* Wing burners
* Whip-finish tool
* Dubbing teaser
* Tweezers
* Padded hackle pliers
* Hackle gauge
* Ruler or scale
* Pumice stone
* Single-edged razor blades

BOBBIN THREADER-CLEANER

If you have a bobbin, it follows that you must have a means of pulling the thread through the tube. A piece of fine wire will do, but the threader-cleaner is ideally suited to the task. It also features a small-diameter rod for reaming out the bobbin tube. With today's pre-waxed threads, this must be done now and then.

HALF-HITCH TOOL

Sometimes we can't execute the whip-finish, and must tie off a fly with a series of half-hitches. This simple tool abets this, and is a genuine fly-saver at such times of emergency.

HACKLE GUARDS

These generally come in a set to accomodate various hook sizes. They slip over the eye of the hook, isolating the head area while finishing processes are executed. They are particularly helpful for flies that have deer hair at the head, such as the Muddler Minnow, and are also great fly-savers when things go awry during the final stages.

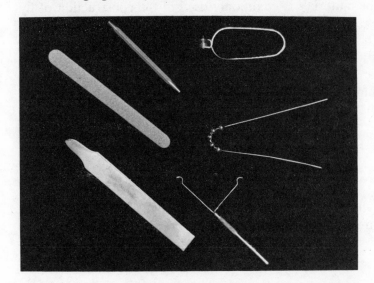

Helpful supplemental tools, clockwise from top: padded-jaw hackle pliers, threader-cleaner (also shown earlier), conventional whip-finish tool, wing burner, emery board for honing hooks, half-hitch tool.

HAIR STACKER

This tool is used to manicure bunches of hair when working on bucktail-style streamers and other types of hairwing flies. The hair is inserted into a cylinder, tips first. Then the stacker is tapped on a table, causing the hairs to become even at the tips. A very helpful device. If you decide not to purchase one initially, use a pill bottle, or something similar.

WING BURNERS

These devices may be purchased individually or in sets to accomodate various hook sizes. They are used for shaping feathers into realistic-looking dry-fly wings. One simply inserts the feather and burns away the excess with a butane lighter or alcohol lamp, not unlike the fletching of an arrow. We used to shape feathers with scissors or nail clippers. Burning is easier, quicker, and produces a uniformly better result.

There are burners for making nymph wing cases. These are okay, although there are other methods I like better. Also, there are ultra-realistic burners which are designed to produce a highly stylized wing, with a leading and trailing edge. For the expert, this can be fun. For the novice, I recommend the less extreme model.

WHIP-FINISH TOOL

The whip-finish knot is used to secure, or tie off, the thread when completing a fly. It is easily executed by hand, as will be taught later in the book. However, some tyers prefer a bit of automation.

I never cared for the whip-finish tool until recently, when Bill Hunter introduced me to the Matarelli whip-finisher. This design represents a breakthrough—the tool is much easier to use than other models. Guess I should buy one.

DUBBING TEASER

Dubbing, either natural fur or synthetic material, is commonly used in the construction of fly bodies. Not infrequently, the effectiveness of such flies is enhanced when the body is teased or fuzzed up a bit. The idea is to do this without cutting the thread or disturbing other components.

The best tool I have found to date is a scroll saw blade, which is available at any hardware store. Select the finest-toothed one you can find and cut it in half. You can even fashion a handle of some sort, if you are so inclined. The blade can be used teeth-up or teeth-down, depending on the specific application. We shall study this technique in the pattern lessons further along.

TWEEZERS

Tweezers are useful for picking up small hooks, holding flies while applying head cement, and similar tasks. This is another common hardware-store item. Most fly shops also sell them.

PADDED HACKLE PLIERS

Padded hackle pliers are available which are shaped differently than the typical models we examined earlier. They also feature a rubber or plastic pad on one or both of the jaws. While not ideally suited to working with small feathers, they are quite useful on larger flies, and as a handle which frees up the fingers for certain preparatory operations on feathers.

HACKLE GAUGE

In the beginning, most tyers have trouble judging hackle size. A hackle gauge is a big help in this area. The *Du Bois* gauge also measures wing length, tail length, and hook size. A most useful item.

RULER OR SCALE

Sometimes it is helpful to measure certain components and materials, particularly when following a set of instructions where measurements are used to describe proportions. I have a small metal scale that has inches and fractions on one side and metric on the other. Very handy.

PUMICE STONE

Rough fingers are the fly-tyer's bane. A pumice stone helps keep them smooth. In extreme cases, an emery board may be used, but with care—the surface is more abrasive than that of a pumice stone.

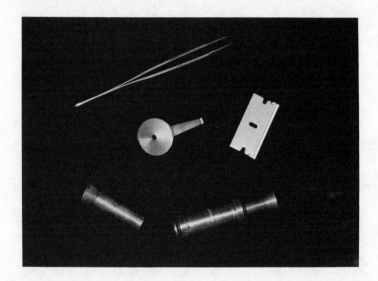

Clockwise from right: common single-edged razor blade, hair stacker with two tubes, hackle guard, tweezers.

SINGLE-EDGED RAZOR BLADES

Sometimes we find it necessary to strip the material from a hook and start over, especially in the earlier stages of our fly-tying careers. A sturdy, single-edged razor blade—the kind my father used for masochism at dawn—is just the thing. A lancet or hobby knife is also suitable, but don't use your scissors—it dulls them.

This completes our study of tools and instruments. However, it is by no means a complete list, as will become apparent with your first mail-order catalog. Many esoteric tools are offered to the fly-tyer—some have merit, others are pure gimmicks. Please heed my advice and don't become a gimmick-junkie. Having taken the pledge, I can speak from experience.

THE BASIC FLY-TYING SET-UP

It's neither possible nor practical to try to prescribe the exact configuration of a fly-tying set-up, because each situation will be different. However, there are a few important features are, or should be, common to all fly-tying set-ups. The most important of these are comfortable seating, proper lighting, easy accessibility of frequently-used items, and proper storage.

SEATING

For brief periods, one can tie flies sitting on anything from a chaise lounge to a log. I have tied flies in my car, with the vise clamped to the steering wheel. But for the long haul, a really good chair provides proper support for the back is recommended.

I have tried a number of chairs, and have settled—if you'll pardon the expression—on an office-type swivel chair with rollers. It is moderately padded, adjustable in height, and flexes with body positioning. Yes, it cost a few bucks, but the comfort more than justifies the expense, and the elimination of orthopedic and chiropractic visits makes the chair a bargain in the long run.

The great thing about the rollers and the swivel feature is ease of mobility. In my den, I am surrounded almost 360 degrees by fly-tying materials and reference books. Being able to roll and rotate facilitates quick access to most of this with minimal effort.

At this writing, a chair like mine costs between $150 and $200, new. In lieu of making that sort of investment early in your fly-tying career, you may opt for a simple straight-backed chair, with or without a modest seat pad, as you prefer. Avoid over-stuffed chairs—they are wonderful for lying around but quite uncomfortable for this sort of work.

THE DESK OR TABLE

The key considerations here are surface area and drawer space. I have a large desk with three drawers on each side. It doesn't happen to have a lap drawer, which I could use. The only negative about a lap drawer is that it interferes with a clamp-type vise mounting. It is possible to use a clamp mount by opening the drawer a couple of inches, if you don't mind trimmings constantly falling into the opening. A pedestal base solves the problem.

I recommend a fairly large work area—you will be surprised how quickly it fills up. For one thing, some of your desk top will probably be devoted to storage of such things as tools and hooks. I use those handy little plastic-drawered cabinets for hooks and certain materials and instruments, and a pegboard for the essential items I use constantly: scissors, bobbins, hackle pliers, and so forth.

You will want a waste basket of some kind. There is a device called a Wastetrol, which mounts on the underside of a desk or table and may be swung out when in use or in for storage. It consists of a frame and a bag. I find it most convenient. However, it is not a "must"—I survived for fifteen years with a three-dollar waste basket.

If I had my way, I would have a plain hardwood or tile floor in my tying room—it makes it much easier to retrieve hooks and flies fall off the desk. Unfortunately, I live in an apartment has wall-to-wall shag carpeting. Trying to find a size 24 hook in a tweed shag rug will do things to one's disposition. One of the most effective methods is to walk the area barefoot, but this I do not recommend.

LIGHTING AND BACKGROUND

In fly-tying, as in dentistry and surgery, it is hardly possible to have too much light. The key is directing the light to illuminate the subject effectively while eliminating shadows and minimizing glare.

I prefer a combination of ambient and focused light. I would love to have a sizeable fluorescent fixture mounted above my tying desk. Unfortunately, I don't think I could sneak that one past the landlord. As a compromise, I have a large extender-arm lamp positioned above my vise and a Tensor focused on the fly itself. Both lamps are attitude-adjustable, so that I can fine-tune as needed.

Can one make do with just a Tensor or similar lamp? Yes, in a well-lit room. But I would counsel against using only a narrowly focused light in a dark room—it causes eyestrain.

The most important factor is to avoid background glare. If lighting is properly arranged, that in itself will minimize reflection. A flat-or semi-flat painted background will work well. It is nice, but not at all essential, to be able to switch colors, in order to optimize for the particular fly being worked on. This can be done without too much difficulty using pieces of mat board, the material used by picture framers. Off-white, grey, and tan are valuable at times, but by far the best all-around shade is pale grey-green. One of the formica companies has a color called "eye-ease green" which is just great. If I were restricted to one shade, that would be it.

STORAGE

At some point in one's fly-tying career, one should obtain a copy of Eric Leiser's book, *Fly-Tying Materials—Their Procurement, Use and Protection*. It contains a wealth of information on taking care of one's precious furs, feathers, and other exotic treasures, plus lots of other helpful tips for the tyer.

With some care, feathers, furs, and fly-tying materials will last for amazingly long periods. I have feathers obtained in the early 1960s through buying out estates, and they are still in good condition. God only knows how long since they were on the bird.

The keys are temperature control, moisture control, and moth protection. This should not present any great problem as normal ambient house temperatures and humidity levels are quite acceptable. The main thing is to avoid exposure to excessive heat or moisture, such as might be caused by a radiator or a damp basement.

Clear plastic boxes make nice storage containers and are readily obtainable. Years ago I had trouble with moth repellent interacting with the plastic, but apparently, that problem has been solved. I do not notice any such interaction in my newer boxes, even though the label on the mothball box warns against contact with plastic. If a chemical-interaction problem is encountered, put the moth balls in a small glass jar with a few holes punched in the lid.

I keep my real treasures—such as expensive capes and wood duck feathers—in cardboard boxes or desk drawers, just in case. Crowding should be avoided, as the material needs to breathe a little. Glass jars with screw-on lids are ideal for some things.

And please, do not forget the mothballs. Just a few in each container will suffice. Eventually they disintegrate as the effective ingredient slowly transforms into a gas, so they must be replenished periodically. Remember that bugs' favorite targets are fur, feathers, and natural wool—be particularly attentive to the protection of those materials.

There is always the threat of introducing some sort of infestation when adding to one's inventory. Materials purchased from reputable dealers have probably been properly cared for. Still, they should be inspected for any signs of insects or larvae and placed in a container with mothballs or crystals.

Materials obtained from noncommercial sources are potential troublemakers, and must be handled accordingly. Most animals carry some form of parasitic insect, or its larvae. Thorough washing in warm water and mild detergent will usually take care of those pests. Rinse carefully and lay the materials out to dry on newspapers, skin side down, if there is a skin side.

To the extent possible, all fatty tissues and grease must be removed. This is done by careful scraping with a stiff-bladed knife, then the detergent bath. The application of a little Boraxo or salt and Boraxo mixture helps, especially in more difficult cases. Allow all materials to remain on the newspaper until thoroughly dry.

In some cases, it is not possible to completely de-grease a pelt or skin. In fact, I sometimes get capes in the mail which are still oozing a little chicken grease. After doing what can be done with scraping, detergent baths, and Boraxo, store such skins in zip-top bags with a piece of blotter next to the skin and a piece of cardboard behind that. Replace the blotter now and then.

Be especially careful of anything which might carry a bit of tissue which cannot be easily excised. Wings of game birds are a prime example. I have hunting friends who supply me with goose wings and such, for which I am most grateful—but they must be properly cared for. The best procedure is to remove the usable quills from a matched pair of wings and keep them together in a plastic bag. However, sometimes we will want the entire wing.

As the American Indians well knew, certain meats can be dried or cured simply by prolonged exposure to air. This is true of game bird wings. Set them aside in matched pairs in a dry area at cool room temperature. Ideally, they should be in the open, but it is okay to put them in a porous, loosely covered container, such as a shoe box. Eventually, the small amount of flesh around the wing bone will cure and become completely dry.

While not an attraction for insects and the like, the colorful, delicate flosses used in fly-tying also deserve a little special care. The main thing is to keep them dust-free and out of prolonged direct light. The drawers in those little cabinets mentioned previously are ideal. They are also good repositories for spools of thread and tinsel.

3

THREADS

I still vividly remember the fascination I felt while watching my grandmother sew. She was a master and took great pride in making beautiful shirts and blouses for the young people in the family. Some operations were done by hand, others at the console of her old Singer treadle-driven sewing machine, which she pedaled with the virtuosity of an E. Power Biggs.

Apparently, my early interest in thread and its applications has carried over. My threads and bobbins are somewhat different than Gramma's, and my patterns are more likely to be found in *Fly Fisherman* magazine than *Good Housekeeping,* but the continual striving to produce a pleasing product remains. I do have a hard time trying to figure out whom I am trying to please—the fish or the fishermen.

Today's fly-tying threads are much better than the ones with which I broke in (no pun intended) back in the 1950s. They are several evolutionary steps beyond what the great nineteenth-century British tyers were forced to use, a fact which has resulted in a revolution in fly-tying methodology.

How so? Pick up a century-old treatise on fly-tying and pay particular attention to the descriptions of threads and the methodology for using them. Often, these threads were procured from commercial tailors and cobblers, along with tacky waxes which were applied to them. The wax served several functions, not the least of which was to make materials stay firmly in place with one or two wraps—could one afford more with those hawsers? I am sure some of the threads I have read about in old fly-tying books had a higher breaking strength than the butt sections of my leaders.

When Pearsall's introduced their "Gossamer Silk"—I can't fix the date—the British tyers must have swooned with ecstasy. So fine, so strong, and all those lovely colors! But by today's standards, their gossamer is hardly that. I still have some—it dates back to the early 1960s—and it is half again the diameter of the common, inexpensive pre-waxed thread I use for most of my tying.

Yes, fellow tyers, today we are blessed with great thread. It is very strong for its fine diameter, is available in a complete range of useful colors, and comes from the manufacturer impregnated with a light wax. I refer, of course, to the universally used synthetic pre-waxed thread, which I would estimate is used at least eighty percent of the time by today's practitioners, myself included.

The typical pre-waxed tying thread currently in vogue is rated 6/0, according to an archaic rating system which I do not begin to understand. My interpretation, based on old books and catalogs, is that "0" was a sort of bench mark. Plain integers designated heavier threads —1, 2, etc. While finer threads were identified as 1/0, 2/0, 4/0, and so forth—the opposite of how hook sizes are designated. What a system!

Our contemporary pre-waxed thread corresponds to the 6/0-rated silk thread of a quarter-century ago. It is pretty fine—about .004 inch in diameter. It is suitable for flies as small as size 22. But the nicest thing about having such strong, fine-diameter thread is that we can make multiple wraps with minimal bulk. That is the key element in the revolution in fly-tying methodology.

I happen to have a few spools of the original pre-waxed thread, which was developed by Herb Howard, a superb fly-dresser from Westchester County, New York. I bought them at an auction following Herb's death in 1971, and it was far from new then. It's the most beautiful stuff—still very strong, and only .003 inch in diameter. How I wish I had a lifetime supply.

Or perhaps I should say I hope I don't have a lifetime supply!

Herb's thread is somewhat different from that which I presently obtain over-the-counter. Herb's was virtually round, like silk thread, and it tended to maintain its shape under tension. The current variety tends toward flatness—or, at least, *some* batches do. I find significant inconsistencies from spool to spool in several essential qualities, specifically:

- Diameter
- Tendency to flatten
- Strength
- Tendency to fray
- Amount of wax

How significant are these? It depends upon how far out-of-specs the thread is, and what it is being used for. If a given spool is slightly on the thick side—.005 inch instead of .004 inch let's say—I can live with that on medium-sized flies, down to a number 16. For anything smaller, I want a finer diameter thread.

The tendency for the thread to flatten is no more than a mild annoyance unless it is extreme. Usually, the flattening is a function of the thread becoming untwisted while the bobbin is suspended between operations, but I do come across batches that are quite flat right off the spool. As with inconsistencies in thread diameter, flattening is not a major problem down to a size 16. Below that, the widening-out effect creates real difficulty.

A marked tendency to flatten has a negative effect on thread strength and increases the tendency of thread to fray. Once the ultra-fine fibres become untwisted, they are individually vulnerable to breakage. Also—and this is my pet peeve—they are much more prone to getting *nicked* by the hook point. A well-manufactured thread—one which is properly twisted and adequately waxed—will probably withstand mild encounters with a hook point, but individual fibres will almost always sever.

I've described several problems which can really cause trouble for the beginning tyer, so I should suggest some solutions. In the case of oversized thread, the only solution is to return it to the dealer. As to the flattening syndrome, try applying some additional wax. Also try re-twisting the thread by spinning the bobbin in the opposite direction from which it turns when suspended. Don't overdo this. If the thread is really incurably flat—and I've encountered that—I would return the spool.

The 6/0 pre-waxed thread is recommended for all of the flies we will study in the pattern lessons, so I will make only brief mention of other threads that I occasionally use. On very large streamers, I may opt for 4/0 or 2/0 nylon. On tiny flies, size 22 and smaller, I will probably use 8/0 silk. There is an ultra-fine synthetic thread on the market called Spiderweb, which gets a lot of hype. Personally, I don't like it. While slightly stronger than 8/0 silk, it flattens drastically—the last thing I want on a number 28 hook shank. It also is kinky and difficult to handle. Waxing helps. Waxing also makes 8/0 silk easier to handle, but it must be done gently.

You will notice another synthetic thread in the shops and catalogs called Monocord. I question the name. To me, "mono" means something consisting of one element—monofilament, for example. Monocord is composed of multiple strands. Oh, well.

Monocord currently comes in two sizes: regular and the heavier "A." The regular is roughly comparable to pre-waxed, but is quite flat by design. It is available waxed or plain. It is quite strong but very slippery. I only use it for a few very specialized operations.

Pre-waxed thread comes in a wide variety of shades from white to black. I don't see that it is necessary to have all of them. The colors I find most useful are white, black, yellow, olive, and brown. I do have others, but these will suffice for the beginner. Actually, one can get away with having only white and black. I did for many years.

My cardinal rule is that I only concern myself with thread color when it shows or when it affects the shading of the materials used in the construction of the fly. Therefore, I would use a pale thread on lighter flies and a dark thread on darker flies. I try to match it to the body color, but a close match isn't necessary as long as the overall coloration of the fly is not affected.

Thread color is much more critical on subsurface flies. When the body becomes saturated with water, thread color will show through, particularly if a dark thread is used under a pale-colored body. Later on, after you've learned to tie a bit, spin some cream-colored fur onto black thread, wrap it onto a hook, and drop it into a glass of water. Do the same thing using white thread. You will see dramatic contrasts.

Black thread is okay under a fairly dark body such as muskrat fur, but, in other cases, I would use a less dominating color. The pattern lessons will enable the student to gain some experience in thread's color effects. If you don't have a particular thread color, use something lighter. For example, you might use white where yellow is called for. When the fly is finished, proper head color can be obtained with a touch from a waterproof felt marker.

Incidentally, it is not always undesirable for the color of the tying thread to contrast with the color of the body material. Attractive effects can be obtained by such artifices as spinning pale cream fur over orange or olive thread. This is a technique with which to experiment as your fly-tying expertise develops.

A few observations pertaining to silk thread as we wrap up this chapter. As stated, I use the standard pre-waxed synthetic thread for almost all of my work, and can see no reason for doing otherwise. However, I do prefer 8/0 silk for my miniatures. While I don't recommend tiny flies—24s, 26s, and smaller—for one's initial efforts, it is quite possible that some tyers will want to learn to dress them fairly early in the game. Mini-flies are so important on certain waters that to be without them is to forfeit the match.

Silk is an organic product subject to gradual decomposition. It is a slow process—I have 8/0 silk that is over ten years old and still usable. However, the fresher it is, the better. Since the clock is ticking away on silk on the dealer's shelf as well as in your thread drawer, it is advisable to test any silk you buy. While 8/0 can't be expected to approximate the strength of everyday pre-waxed, it should be able to support the weight of the bobbin and allow the tyer to perform normal operations without breakage.

I expect there will be some wonderful developments in thread in future years. Actually, I'm surprised we haven't seen more of these already. The last big breakthrough was the 6/0 pre-waxed. That was fifteen years ago, at this writing, and the original product was better than the mass-produced stuff we get today. That ain't progress, guys and gals.

Recently a new thread was introduced which shows promise for applications where very strong thread is required. The name is Kevlar. It is similar to Monocord in appearance and handling characteristics; it tends toward flatness and is very slippery. It is also unbelievably strong—in fact, I can't break it without putting gloves on. By the time this book is in publication, I would expect that Kevlar will be in wide use for large streamers, saltwater flies, bass bugs, and flies which use flared-and-trimmed deer hair, such as the Muddler.

4

HOOKS

One of the nice things about fly-tying today is that good-quality hooks can be obtained readily and inexpensively. Presently, this is attributable to the work of two companies: O. Mustad and Sons of Oslo, Norway, and Partridge of Redditch, England. I would not rule out the possible emergence of other competitors as growth creates an increasingly attractive market.

Mustad is considerably the larger of the two firms. It manufactures an enormous variety of hooks, suitable for everything from tuna fishing to the most minute dry-fly tying. Mustad's model 94840 is the Chevrolet of the fly-tying universe—inexpensive, of reasonably good quality, ubiquitous. Primarily a dry-fly hook, it may be used for wet flies where reduced weight is desirable.

Partridge, as far as its exports to the United States are concerned, directs its efforts toward producing a limited number of models for the fly-tying market. The emphasis is on quality control and hook design. I particularly like their dry-fly hooks and salmon-fly hooks, which are in a class by themselves.

Let us first consider hook design from the standpoint of the type of fly for which a particular hook is appropriate. This brings into play several major considerations:
- Heaviness or thickness of wire
- Length of shank
- Length of point and size of barb

There are some other criteria which, while worth considering, are secondary—design of bend and design of eye are two which readily come to mind. We will address these subsequently.

In the illustration, we see a selection of hooks most commonly used in fly-tying, along with a typical baitfishing hook. A number of striking differences are apparent. The bait hook—which, incidentally, is not manufactured by either Mustad or Partridge—features heavy wire, a long point that curves inward, and a large barb. I believe a certain amount of eye-appeal is incorporated in this design, as it is quite lethal-looking. The heavy wire, long point, and large barb presuppose the use of tackle of sufficent strength to allow the angler to strike with considerable force. The heavier the wire, the longer the point, the larger the barb, the greater the force required to effectively impale the fish.

The dry-fly hook features fine wire, a relatively short point, and a delicate barb. The fine wire is used to minimize weight, thereby enhancing floatability. The hook's penetration characteristics

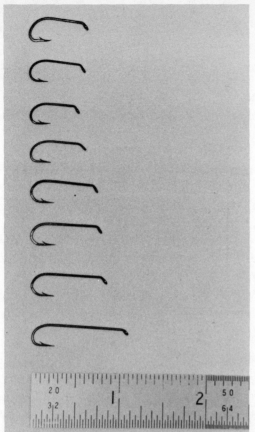

From top to bottom: typical bait hook, standard dry-fly hook (Mustad 94840), standard wet-fly hook (Mustad 3906), 1X long (Mustad 3906B), 2X long (Mustad 9671), 3X long (Mustad 9672), 4X long (Mustad 79580) and 6X long (Mustad 3664A). These are size 10 hooks.

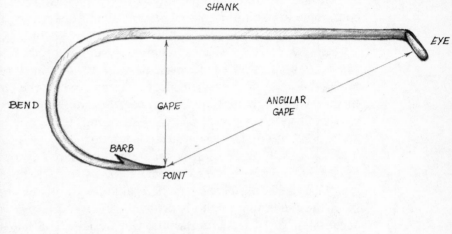

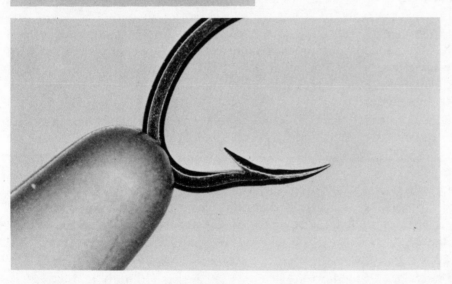

Close-up of barb and point of bait hook—not well suited for fly tying.

are enhanced by the fine, sharp point and minimal barb. This is important, as dry flies are usually fished with a fine leader tippet, which will not tolerate an overly forceful strike.

The standard wet-fly hook is quite similar to the standard dry, except that heavier wire is employed. This serves the dual purpose of causing the fly to sink and allowing a heavier leader tippet to be used. Quite frequently, a fish takes a subsurface fly as the line straightens, thereby causing more strain on the terminal tackle and making a somewhat heavier tippet desirable. This is particularly true in faster water, where strikes are often unexpected and jolting.

The progressively longer hooks are used to create different proportions or silhouettes, as dictated by the type of insect or baitfish the fly is designed to simulate. For example, certain nymphs are quite elongated in shape. To create effective imitations, we use hooks with shank lengths of 1X to 4X, as the pattern lessons will demonstrate.

Basically, there are three hook dimensions that we need be concerned with:
• Size of the gape
• Shank length
• Wire diameter

Somehow, the numbering plans used to define these dimensions have managed to escape the attention of the international standards people. There needs to be an improved system that can be commonly applied to hooks of *all* manufacture. Lacking that, we are left to struggle with a rather antiquated and subjective British hook-rating system.

Very well. Hook size, as commonly understood, relates to the size of the gape. Using the Mustad 94840 as an example—I hesitate to use the term "standard"—we see that on a size 12 hook, the gape measures 3/16 inches (5 mm), while the shank length measures 3/8 inches (10 mm). From this, we can see that on a standard-shank hook, the shank length is twice the gape. This may vary a bit with size, but practically speaking, it may be considered a constant as far as the 94840 and hooks of similar design are concerned.

Now let's look at what is generally considered to be a "standard" wet-fly hook, the Mustad model 3906. The gape measurement for a size 12 is the same as the 94840, and so is the overall length of the hook. However, the usable length of the shank, which I define as being the distance from the beginning of the bend to the rear of the eye, is only about 5/16 inches (8 mm). This is accounted for by a slight variation in design. The 94840 incorporates an approximation of the model perfect design, in which the bend is a semicircle. The 3906 uses a sproat design, in which the bend is a compound curve. The wet fly hook has a 1/16 inch shorter shank.

We can see that usable shank length may vary with hook design. The Mustad model 3906B hook is listed as having a 1X-long shank. It measures the same as the 94840. Therefore, if we want to tie a wet fly which is the same length as a particular dry fly tied on a Mustad 94840, we must either use a 1X-shank hook (3906B) or a size larger standard-shank hook (3906). Or we can select a hook of another model or manufacture.

I realize this is confusing, and I strongly feel the hook-manufacturing industry owes fly-tyers a large apology for the lack of standards. We should be aware of the true size of the hooks we purchase and use.

Generally, hooks of the 94840 type are used for all common dry-fly sizes, so a modicum of standardization is thus obtained. In the case of subsurface flies, we frequently vary the shank length to obtain the desired proportions, as mentioned earlier. Therefore, let us compare apples to apples, and examine the relative shank lengths of some popular wet-fly/nymph/streamer hooks, using the 3906 as a bench mark.

Size	Model	Rated Shank Length	Measured Shank Length
10	3906	Standard	12/32 inches (10 mm)
10	3906B	1X long	15/32 " (12 mm)
10	9671	2X long	17/32 " (14 mm)
10	9672	3X long	19/32 " (15 mm)
10	79580	4X long	21/32 " (17 mm)
10	3665A	6X long	28/32 " (22 mm)

Here is the decimal expression of the above:

3906	1.0	9672	1.58
3906B	1.25	79580	1.75
9671	1.42	3665A	2.33

Allowing for slight variations in design and production, and considering that there is no 5X shank length, the progression of sizes is sufficiently linear so that we can feel reasonably secure purchasing hooks in the fly shop without ruler in hand. If I were to sample many batches of these hooks over a period of time and take the mean, I might reduce the nonlinearity a bit, but to what end? We now have sufficient background to select the hooks we shall use for the patterns in the book, plus a great many others.

There is also a rating system which describes wire diameter, or more accurately, relative wire thickness. It is even more poorly conceived than the shank-length system. Fortunately, we need learn only a couple of major points.

Hook manufacturers use wire of appropriate diameter for the particular size and type of hook. Unless I have something very special in mind, such as tying flies for Alaska, I don't get overly concerned with wire thickness. However, there are a few options with dry-fly hooks which warrant attention.

Mustad refers to the 94840 as having 1X-fine wire—here we go with the digit-Xs again! A size 14 measures .018 inch in diameter. Mustad makes a model 94833 which they describe as 3X-fine, which measures .016 inch on the micrometer. The Partridge T0530 is described by the manufacturer as 4X-fine. It "mikes" .017 inch. All this does is to verify the fact that the rating system is *no* system at all.

If we were to accept the Mustad 94840 1X-fine wire as standard—and I can justify that only on the grounds that it is overwhelmingly the most widely used dry-fly hook in the world—and we accept their 3X-fine designation, then the Partridge has to be 2X-fine. But that's not fair to Partridge—if Mustad can use a rating system which is relevant only to its own product line, so can Partridge! Amusing, yes?

Okay, what are we really concerned with here? Wire diameter affects two factors: hook strength and hook weight, or actually, floatation. Personally, I am not willing to trade off a modest gain in floatation for a significant sacrifice in strength. I have had some disheartening experiences over the years with 94833s being straightened or broken by fish. I do sometimes use them for special-purpose flies. More and more I favor the Partridge, which seems to offer a good compromise when delicacy is wanted.

In describing the style of bends used on various hooks, I have used the terms *model-perfect* and *sproat*. I will introduce a third, the *limerick*. These three styles pretty well cover the types of bends commonly employed in fly hooks today.

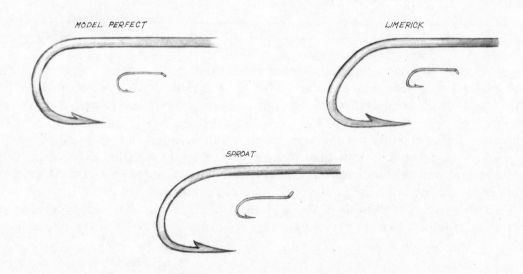

The *model-perfect* bend, or *round* bend, is a semicircle, or approximately so. It is favored for the dry fly, because the more abrupt curvature tends to counter any tendency one might have to run the tying thread too far to the rear, forcing the tail of the fly to angle downward.

The *sproat* bend employs a compound curve, with the bend starting as a gentle curve and becoming progressively more acute. It is generally considered to be more aesthetically pleasing on wet flies than the model perfect. On a functional level, it permits the manufacturer to use a slightly longer point, which I consider to be mildly advantageous in certain respects and mildly disadvantageous in others. Essentially, it is a non-issue unless the point is extremely oversized.

The *limerick* bend is considered classic for streamers, and I must admit to a great fondness for it. Here, the compounding of the curve is greater than with the sproat, producing a rather spear-like point. I feel this is overdone on certain models, to the extent that too much force is required to drive the point home. I modify these hooks with a tiny file or stone, which both sharpens the point and slightly reduces its length. It is not a good idea to shorten the point very much, how-ever, because it then becomes too stubby and doesn't penetrate well.

We also have three distinct designs for the eye of the hook: *turned-down*, *turned-up*, and *straight*, or *ringed*. For general tying, I prefer the turned-down eye. Ringed-eye hooks are nice for certain streamers. I also favor them for tiny dry flies, where the turned-down eye actually tends to shield the point, reducing hooking effectiveness. The ringed-eye hook has better *angular-gape* characteristics than the turned-down eye, which is critical below size 20. We won't be tying any flies that small in this book, but at some point you will probably need to master mini-flies, as they can be tremendously effective.

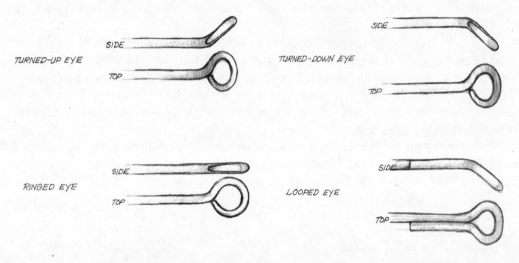

Having discovered the ringed-eye, I no longer use turned-up-eye hooks, except for Atlantic salmon flies, where it is considered classic to use the black-finished, turned-up-looped-eye hook. The reason is that they do not accomodate the several leader knots I use as well as do the other two designs.

While on the subject of hook eyes, I want to make the reader aware of a quality-control problem that all of us encounter from time to time. It has to do with the eye not being fully closed—that is, not forming a complete ring. Better-quality hooks taper the wire used to form the eye, resulting in a neat eye with the least possible bulk. A machine bends the wire into a 360-degree loop, with the tip coming flush to the very front of the shank. On occasion, production failures occur, and complete closure of the eye is not obtained, as shown in the illustration.

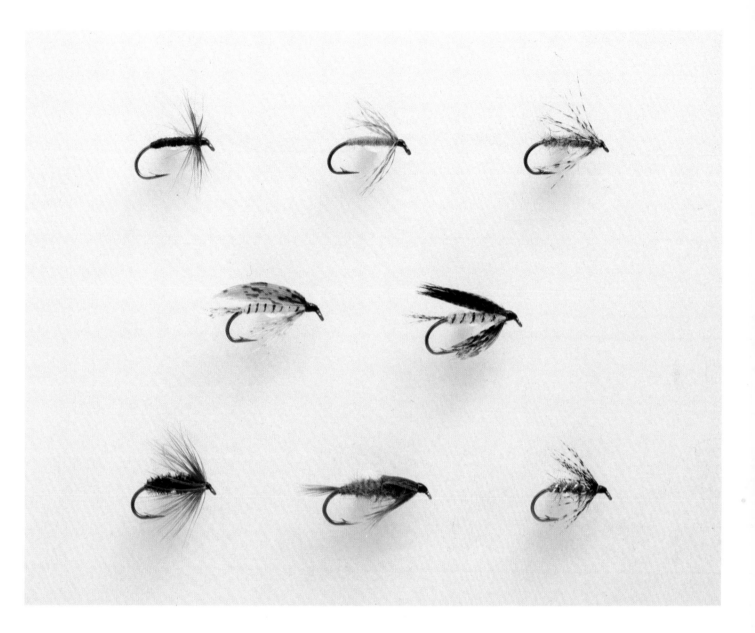

WET FLIES

Basic Black   Olive/Grouse   Fur/Grouse—Plain

March Brown—   March Brown—
Turkey Wing   Mallard Wing

Brown Hackle   Muskrat Nymph   Fur/Grouse—G.R.

All color photographs by Dee Weidig

STREAMERS

Wooly Worm	Wooly Bugger
Mickey Finn—Plain, Bucktail	Mickey Finn—Optic, Craft Fur
Golden Darter— Marabou	Golden Darter— Feather Wing

DRY FLIES

Blue-Winged Olive   Hair-Wing Royal Coachman   Foxy Quill

Dun Variant

Hair-Wing Caddis—
Trimmed

Hair-Wing Caddis—
Palmered

Hair-Wing Caddis—
Front Hackle

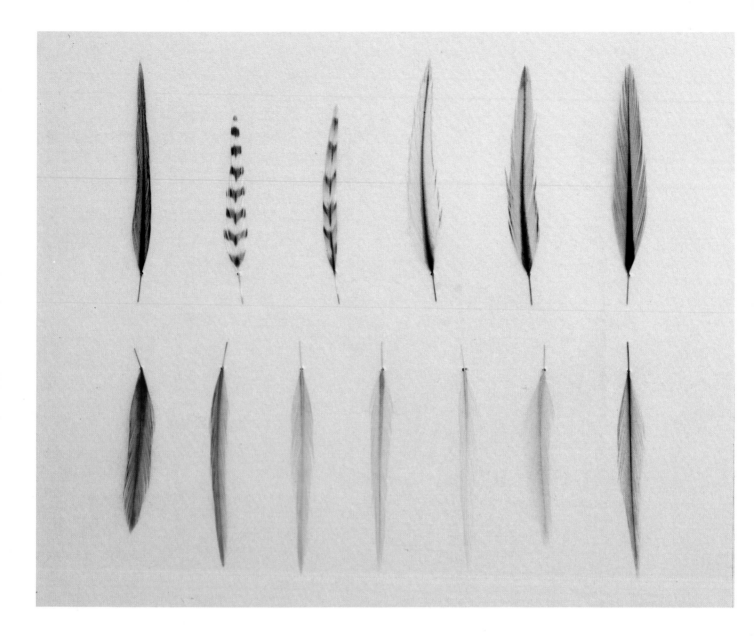

DRY-FLY HACKLES

Top Row: Black, Grizzly, Cree, Light Badger, Golden Badger, Furnace

Bottom Row: Dark Brown, Fiery Brown, Ginger, Straw Cream, Cream, Dun, Dark Dun

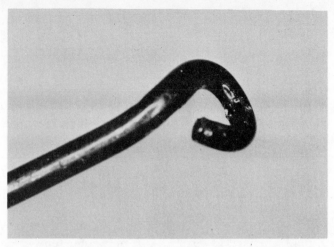

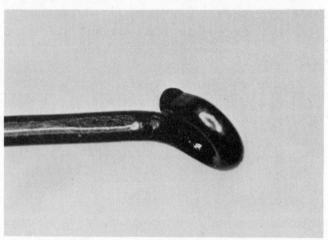

Two examples of malformed eyes.

This is a serious problem, and I strongly recommend that any hook which is thus malformed be discarded. You will have trouble finishing off the head, because the tying thread will slip into the eye area. Worse, the fly will probably slip off the leader if one attempts to fish with it. Get into the habit of checking the eye as you mount a hook in your vise. If you encounter more than one or two such hooks in a box, take a quick look at the rest, or at least enough of them for a valid sample, as they may be part of a bad batch and should be returned.

I do *not* recommend closing the loop by using pliers. Usually, the wire will break, but even if it doesn't, you may have weakened or cracked it. In a pinch, you might get away with closing an eye on a larger streamer or wet-fly hook, these being stronger and not so brittle as a dry-fly hook, but I still don't recommend the practice.

A quality issue related to the eye of the hook has to do with proper location of the eye. On turned-down-eye hooks, we sometimes encounter ones with the front of the shank bent downward ahead of the eye, as in the illustration. This may cause problems with the leader knot and may also cause poor hook engagement. If this condition is severe and prevalent in a box of hooks, ask for a replacement.

Another quality issue concerns the wire used in manufacturing the hooks. Occasionally a bad batch slips through the manufacturer's quality-control checks, resulting in a run of hooks which are either too soft or too brittle. This is particularly critical in dry-fly hooks and is especially serious in the 3X-fine models.

If you should notice either of two propensities in hooks out of a particular box, you may have a bad batch. These are:

• Hook bends too easily during fly-tying. It may actually bend from the weight of the bobbin alone.
• Hook breaks while being clamped into the vise.

Test a few more hooks. If they manifest the problem consistently, return the box. Your dealer will probably not be shocked; he is probably seeing other returns because your hooks would be part of a larger run. Just make sure the replacements are of proper quality.

SHARPENING

I have yet to see a hook come direct from the factory that couldn't stand improvement by discreet sharpening. Some hooks are far worse than others. Larger hooks in particular tend to be rather dull.

A very fine-grit stone, such as an Arkansas stone, is excellent for hook sharpening. Diamond and ceramic sharpeners are also very good. In a pinch, you can use an emery board—you won't get many sharpenings from a board, as the hooks score them.

Mounting the hook in your fly-tying vise when sharpening makes it easy. Stroke toward the point, and try to work mainly on the sides and inside of the point. It's okay to touch up the outside a little, but take care to avoid rounding it inward too much—you will reduce the hook's engagement characteristics.

DE-BARBING

It is wise to de-barb a hook *before* tying a fly on it. Now and then a point will break off during de-barbing, and labor and materials are lost if a fly is already in place.

De-barbing can be accomplished either by pinching or filing. Filing is safer from the standpoint of potential damage, but pinching is allowable if done properly.

Mount the hook in the vise when using the filing method. Use only the very finest miniature file or stone. Simply file away the barb without exerting too much pressure. If you also intend to sharpen the hook, this is the time to do it.

For the pinching method, you will need a pair of fine-nosed pliers. Gently pinch down the very tip of the barb. It will flatten or break off, either of which is okay. Don't try to flatten the small bump which remains—that's the way hooks get broken. If a perfectly flat point is desired, use the filing method.

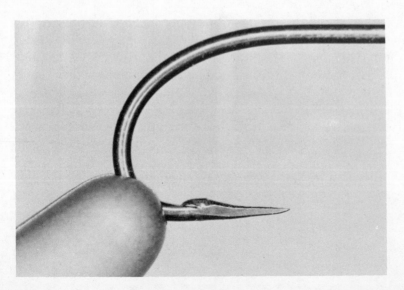

A bent-down barb.

At this point, you may be asking yourself, "Why would anyone de-barb a hook? Would the manufacturer bother to create the barb in the first place if it wasn't absolutely essential to prevent the point from slipping out?" With fly hooks, smaller ones in particular, I am convinced a barbless hook will hold at least as well as a barbed one. Better penetration is often achieved, and less tissue disturbance during the playing of a fish takes place.

And, of course, the purpose of all this is the effortless and safe release of fish. Many premium-quality waters now have regulations which prohibit or severely limit the killing of fish. This, plus a growing disinclination among today's sport fishermen and women to kill fish even where it is legal has saved public fishing. Still, far too many fish are killed by the unthinking and uncaring. I hope social and regulatory pressures will effect even greater reductions in creeled fish in the future.

5

MATERIALS AND COMPONENTS

To the dedicated fly-tyer, the world is one great big fly-tying-materials warehouse. I find myself gazing covetously at my friends' pets, visualizing their pelts and tails tied to hook shanks. Sometimes I draw reproving glares as I ogle women's fur coats in an elevator, oblivious to the wearer inside it. How could they understand? And heaven forbid I should be allowed inside a chicken yard—temptation might overwhelm me!

Seriously, the universe of fly-tying materials, while perhaps not infinite, is vast. The creative tyer will spend his or her entire life in discovery and innovation. In this chapter, we will develop an orientation in the more common materials, such as we will use in the pattern lessons. This will be expanded upon in the lessons themselves.

BODY MATERIALS

Let us first examine the most prolific category, that being body materials. It includes everything from plain old thread to exotic furs and feathers. Here is a partial listing:
- Yarns, natural and synthetic
- Furs, natural, dyed, and synthetic
- Quills obtained from feathers
- Floss, produced expressly for fly-tying
- Tinsel (not the Christmas variety)
- Chenille
- Herl

These materials are used by themselves or in combination. For example, a floss or fur body may be augmented with a ribbing of tinsel in order to add a little "flash."

Let's study each type of material, with particular attention to the characteristics which would influence the tyer to use that particular material on a given fly pattern.

YARNS

Wool yarn was one of man's earliest inventions as a material for making clothing. It is not surprising that the earliest recorded fly-tying mentions its use.

As any knitter can attest, yarns vary a great deal. Some are rough and coarse, some soft and smooth, some luxuriant with long fibres. Some are extremely heavy or thick, such as the coarse crewel wool used in Scandinavian sweaters. Others are quite thin or fine, such as the mending yarn found on cards in fabric or handcraft stores. Each has its place in fly-tying.

Crewel wool is used in the construction of larger wet flies and nymphs—prime examples are imitations of the enormous stonefly nymphs common to many western rivers. Its main attributes are thickness and soft texture, which enable the tyer to cover a very large hook quickly and evenly.

While crewel wool may be dyed, it is often used as it comes from the sheep. The colors range from white to black, with many subtle shades of brown and grey in between. I particularly favor the natural shades because they are not "flat," as dyed colors often are. They are a composite of a number of shades, similar to the way stream insects are colored by nature.

As with most yarns, crewel wool is usually composed of two or more twisted strands. The fly-tyer may use one individual strand or more, depending on the size and thickness of the body being constructed.

The more refined, less-thick wool yarns are sometimes used for smaller fly bodies. A great variety of dyed colors are available, also some interesting natural and combination shades which have a mottled or "tweedy"cast. These I particularly like.

Wool yarn is not noted for having good natural floatation. Today, we can get almost anything to float using modern chemical floatants. However, wool yarns are recommended primarily for work on wet flies.

Synthetic yarns utilize various materials, with new ones popping up all the time—thus, their characteristics are far more diversified than wool. Some are labeled with generic names which tell us something of their nature, such as orlon or polypropylene. Others use brand names which provide few clues as to the actual material.

Perhaps the most important attribute of synthetic yarns is that they tend to float much better than wool. This varies, of course, I find it difficult to determine which ones actually float best, because a "pure" test is virtually impossible, given labeling obscurities. I can say that the acrylics and polypropylenes are satisfactory in their floatation properties.

There has been a lot of hype in recent years that certain synthetic materials will make a fly float like a cork. I've not found this to be totally true. A great deal depends on how the material is applied to the hook. While certain synthetic fibres may not absorb water, a capillary effect occurs when a great many of them are compressed into a mass, as in the case of a fly body.

One nice thing about synthetic bodies, and this applies to both yarn and fur, is that when it has absorbed some water, it gives it up easily. This is particularly true of polypropylene. A good squeeze renders a fly virtually dry, and a quick treatment with a dessicant and a floatant completely restores its properties of floatation.

Another attribute of certain synthetics is their brilliance of color. Some have a touch of glitter (sparkle yarns), others are highly fluorescent. While such brilliance is not always appropriate, there are circumstances where it is just the thing for attracting the attention of indifferent fish.

FURS

As mentioned, fly-tyers use both natural and synthetic furs. Sometimes, the synthetics are not labeled as fur in the materials catalogs—rather, they are called body materials or *dubbing*.

Dubbing is one of the oldest terms in the fly-tying vocabulary. It can be a noun: "The body in this pattern is made of synthetic dubbing," or a verb: "The tyer is now dubbing the body." For purposes of this discussion, materials that are applied using the dubbing method will be considered furs.

As with wools, natural furs manifest subtle, complex colorations which can be effectively employed to simulate the elusive colors of the insects fish feed upon. A most notable example is the Hendrickson pattern described in Art Flick's classic, *New Streamside Guide to Naturals and Their Imitations*. Art noticed the subtle pinkish cast of a particular mayfly indigenous to his home streams, and used urine-stained fur from a vixen red fox to obtain the shade. Not an easy item to come by.

Natural furs also vary greatly in texture, ranging from soft and fine to coarse and springy. Each has its applications. Certain coarse furs, while rather difficult to work with, produce wonderfully translucent bodies. I recall my early struggles with seal hair and polar bear underfur. Until a modicum of skill was developed, it was like dubbing with the bristles off a toothbrush. However, it was well worth the effort.

Incidentally, this text mentions the use of materials from certain animals, such as seal and polar bear, that I realize may raise some sensitive issues. Let me state that I am not in favor of the indiscriminate killing of any animal, be it scarce or not, and I don't know of any fly-tyers who are. On the other hand, I'm not anti-hunting either—in fact, I'm known to blow a few holes in the sky each autumn, while grouse fly off through the trees. I think it's entirely a matter of discretion, self-control, education, legality, and sensitivity.

Today we are fortunate in that many excellent synthetic substitutes are available, some of which are actually superior to the real thing. Also, certain domestic animals which are raised for food provide us materials which serve as acceptable replacements for exotics. This allows fly-tyers to practice our craft with a clear conscience.

Back on the subject of natural furs, you will find that virtually all of them contain guard hairs. These are the longer, stiffer fibres which provide protective coloration for the animal and protection for the soft underfur. Sometimes both the guard hairs and underfur are used, other times just the underfur, and in a few cases, just the guard hairs. It is easy to separate the two—we will learn how in the pattern lessons.

With the evolution of synthetics, natural furs are used less and less these days. However, there are some I definitely wouldn't want to be without, as they make really terrific bodies. These include Australian opossum, rabbit, red fox squirrel, woodchuck, and hare's mask.

Australian opossum is a soft, long-fibred fur that is easy to work with. The coloration ranges from pale grey to cream to amber to tan and rust. It makes a great substitute for red fox—in fact, I prefer it.

Rabbits come in every conceivable shade from white to black. The soft underfur is wonderfully easy to work with, especially after it has been fluffed up in a fur blender. Some pelts contain a vast array of shades, and guard hairs which produce a beautiful rough, mottled effect. All types of rabbits have some useful fur, particularly the large Belgian, European, and Australian strains.

Typical piece of natural fur, showing guard hairs and under fur.

White rabbit fur is very easy to dye in bright colors, and it keeps its easy workability.

The fox squirrel is very common throughout the Midwest. It is a large animal as squirrels go, with a gorgeous, long-haired tail, which is used on many streamer and salmon-fly patterns. The body fur varies from a fiery tan in the belly to a mottled grey-tan on the back. Marvelous effects can be obtained by mixing these shades.

Woodchuck, to my knowledge, is not commercially available, although I don't believe there is any restriction on its sale. The animal proliferates in the Northeast, where I live, and it is easy to obtain a limitless supply simply by picking up fresh road-kills. It is a miserably difficult beast to skin, and he who would thus obtain a pelt is in for a lot of cutting, pulling, scraping, Boraxing, and salting.

But, oh! Is it worth the trouble! The underfur offers a rich variety of tans, rusts, and greys—each pelt is different. While coarse, the fur is not that hard to use, and its natural oiliness makes it an excellent floater, great for larger dry flies. And, the guard hairs are terrific for hair-wings, both wet and dry. Tyers of Atlantic salmon flies use them as a substitute for grey fox in the Rat series.

A prime hare's mask affords the tyer more useful body material than perhaps any other single source. This is where we obtain the rough, tweedy dubbing for the famed Hare's Ear, a very ancient and incredibly effective pattern. If a man had a hare's mask, some grouse hackle, and a variety of hooks from size 10 to 18, he could keep himself in trout with no problem.

Hare's masks are readily available at modest prices. Try to select a large, mature mask from a European or Australian hare, with lots of sandy-colored fuzz on the ears and face, and plenty of guard hairs. Packaged mixtures in natural and dyed shades are now available. Some look very interesting, but they appear to have a lot of body fur mixed in. Sometimes it is necessary and desirable to mix in a little body fur or supplementary guard hair, but I like to keep my hare's mask dubbing as pure as possible.

Of course, there are other furs not mentioned here which are quite useful, and you may find some which will give you pleasing results. Experiment to your heart's content—there are no hard and fast rules.

Synthetic furs are a comparatively new entry in the materials derby. We began to see them in the catalogs soon after the beginning of the great fly-fishing boom, around 1970. They immediately became popular, even though the early products left much to be desired. Despite deficiencies in texture and fibrosity, the new synthetics offered tyers a wide variety of useful shades and were quite inexpensive.

Evolution in synthetic materials has progressed at an accelerated pace, and I'm sure it will continue. Synthetics mixtures were introduced which offered life-like colors and more workable textures. One of my favorites at this writing is the Spectrum by Andra Co. The Spectrum assortment of colors shows a great deal of attention to the coloration of various stream insects. It is fine-fibre, soft dubbing, eminently suitable for delicate dry flies.

Another current product I particularly like is Ligas, by Creative Anglers. It is advertised as an ultra-translucent nymph blend, and it certainly is that, but I see no reason why it couldn't be used effectively in certain dry-fly applications. The forty colors available at this writing are very well-conceived—someone has done their homework. While resembling seal's hair, the material is easily workable and has a wonderful sparkle. It is the right stuff.

Before taking pen in hand, I had promised myself to minimize the use of brand names in this book, and I will keep that covenant. However, I find it difficult to avoid mention of products that have particularly distinguished themselves, and feel I would be doing both those outstanding suppliers and my readers a disservice if I kept everything totally generic. My apologies to any worthy manufacturers not mentioned, past, present, and future.

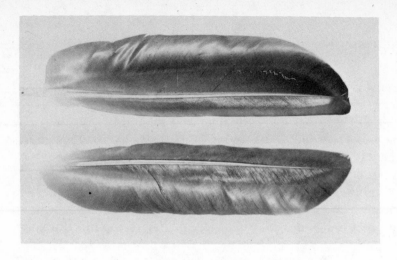

A matched pair of goose secondary wing feathers, or quills.

Quills

Several types of quills are commonly used in fly-tying. Mainly, they are employed in the construction of dry flies to produce a neat, smooth, and reasonably buoyant body.

Two quills are particularly popular:
- Center quills from a chicken feather with the fibers stripped off
- Quills from a peacock tail, with the herl removed

Some of the most famous and attractive dry flies in history call for one or the other of these quills. The list includes the Quill Gordon, the Red Quill, the Cahill Quill, the Olive Quill, and Art Flick's three Variants—the Dun, Cream, and Grey Fox. Both quills are very easy to prepare and apply, as we shall learn later on.

Floss

Fly-tying floss is quite different from dental hygiene floss. It is a soft, very pliable material which, when wrapped around the hook shank, produces a smooth, slick body.

At one time, floss was extremely popular for both wet-fly and dry-fly bodies. Its popularity has diminished considerably, for a number of reasons:
- It is not as durable as dubbing. The body tends to become frayed with use.
- It does not have the translucency and complexity of coloration that dubbing has and is consequently not as effective.
- When used for dry flies, floss does not float well.

Floss comes in a wonderful array of colors and shades, including some hot fluorescent colors. It is available in different thicknesses to accommodate a range of fly sizes. A four-stranded weave permits the tyer to use one to four strands to obtain the desired bulk.

Originally, all floss was made of silk. Today, synthetics have largely replaced silk, and though I am a traditionalist in certain respects, I readily admit that the new synthetics are just great. The colors are brilliant and enduring, and the material packs onto the hook smoothly and neatly. The multiple strands can easily be separated and used individually or in groups of two or three where a slim effect is wanted.

During my fly-tying career I have used floss made of various synthetics, including nylon, dacron, rayon, and acetate. Of these, rayon takes the prize. Rayon has all of the properties one would desire in a floss—brilliance, color-fastness, and ease and smoothness of application. I have a piece on my desk which I find is composed of nine individual strands, twisted loosely together. Each strand has sufficient tensile strength to be used by itself, and the material does not fray too badly when I pull the strands apart. This is important to me because I tie many salmon flies and decorative brook trout patterns, some on rather small hooks.

Acetate floss has an interesting property. When dipped in Acetone, the floss softens for a moment and allows the tyer to alter the shape of the fly body. I frequently use acetate floss as an underbody because I can dip it in Acetone and squeeze it flat with pliers to obtain an attractive silhouette for nymphs. Then, I cover it with dubbing or some other type of body material.

It appears at this writing that silk floss may be on the way out, based on the Pearsall Co.'s announcement that they were discontinuing their line of flosses. That's akin to Goodyear dropping out of the tire business. Traditionalists will mourn the passing of silk—if indeed it completely disappears from the market—but the replacements are so good that it will not be missed for long.

Even synthetic flosses will eventually fade a bit, and all flosses tend to gather dust, so keep your spools covered and away from prolonged direct light. I keep mine in one of those little multi-drawered cabinets used for nuts, bolts, screws, etc.

I've mentioned Eric Leiser's *Fly-Tying Materials*. This book contains a wealth of information on how to safeguard one's delicate treasures from the ravages of insects, moisture, and decomposition. Topics such as dyeing, bleaching, cleaning, and conditioning of animal and bird skins are covered in great detail. As Art Flick says in the introduction, "Bless you, Eric Leiser! You have done all fly-tyers a real service."

Tinsel

To the fly-tyer, tinsel is much more than something which gets dragged out after Thanksgiving and put away after New Year's. Of course, Christmas tinsel bears little resemblance to fly-tying tinsel, other than that they both sparkle. And that is the purpose of tinsel—to add flash or sparkle to certain flies and lures.

While others are available, by far the most widely used tinsel colors are silver and gold. Mylar tinsel provides both for the price of one—gold on one side and silver on the other.

There are three major types of tinsel—flat, oval, and embossed. Flat tinsel is simply an unmarked narrow ribbon of metallic-appearing material. Oval tinsel is braided over a fine thread core, and is indeed oval in shape. Embossed, the third common type of tinsel, is similar in appearance to oval but does not have a core—embossed markings are pressed into the material. Because it has no core, embossed tinsel has less tensile strength than oval and so is not available in very small diameters. Still, it is useful for certain applications.

Why three types of tinsel? There are reasons which relate to highly sophisticated and stylized schools of tying, and are not appropriate for a basic book. As regards the applications we will examine in later chapters, where both will be used, perhaps tradition and appearance are the main considerations. I have read that embossed and oval tinsels effect a different *light pattern*—remember that term, you will hear it constantly in fly-fishing circles. Supposedly, the variegated surface reflects many little pinpoints of light, which is suggestive of certain natural phenomena. Perhaps. I can't capture the effect on film. Could be my photography.

Tinsel is sometimes used by itself to form a sparkly body, but more often it is used as ribbing to add flash to a body composed of some other material. It *can* make a difference—I have been able to satisfy myself on that point. There have been days when the fish were selective to flies with tinsel ribbing. There were also days when they were selective to nonribbed flies, days when they would take both, and days when they would take neither. One must experiment.

Tinsel comes in a variety of widths, to accommodate a range of hook sizes and applications. Some types are simply labeled heavy, medium, fine, etc., and it is up to the tyer to select the appropriate size. Other types are graded by hook size: 10, 12, 14, 16/18, etc. I do not always agree with the manufacturer in this respect. I am particularly conservative as regards the width of tinsel used for ribbing. I like it narrow because I am trying merely to add a touch of sparkle, and I want the basic body color to predominate.

There is also a material called braided mylar tubing which has become quite popular as an alternative to tinsel on larger flies, particularly streamers with weighted bodies. Like many fly-tying materials, it is a by-product of the clothing industry, where it is used as decorative piping. In fact, it can be purchased in most fabric stores. We will see how mylar tubing is used in one of the pattern lessons.

CHENILLE

"Chenille" is French for caterpillar, and the resemblance is immediately apparent. It is a fuzzy material, consisting of short fibres locked in place by a twisted double-thread core. The method of construction is quite similar to the spinning-loop dubbing technique, which we will study in the pattern lessons.

As with most materials, chenille comes in various thicknesses and a wide array of colors. It is inexpensive, simple to use, and makes wonderfully fuzzy bodies. Some extremely important flies utilize chenille, notably the Wooly Worm, the Wooly Bugger, the Montana nymph, and the Girdle Bug.

HERL

Herl is the fuzz found on certain feathers. It is quite thick and pronounced on large feathers, such as ostrich and peacock plumes, but is also present on much smaller feathers. A British river-keeper named Frank Sawyer immortalized himself by developing a simple but deadly nymph, using fibers from a cock pheasant tail wrapped around the hook so that the herl produced a fuzzy, translucent effect.

For the typical fly-tyer, by far the most important herl-producing feather is peacock tail. Many great patterns utilize this material. Fish seem to love it. Fortunately, these feathers naturally fall from the bird during molt, making them a replenishable resource and keeping the price reasonable.

There is virtually no limit to the list of materials that might be used for fly bodies. You will become familiar with others as your tying skills develop. But that's enough for now—let's move on to another category.

WING MATERIALS

This is a much smaller family of materials, even counting innovations spawned by the fly-tying renaissance. I have not found many contemporary materials that pleased me, and consequently have incorporated few of them in my inventory. Innovations in techniques for using traditional wing materials have been more fruitful, but that's for later on, when we get into the pattern lessons.

The following is a listing of some important and popular materials used for making wings:
• Flank feathers—wood duck, mallard, teal, etc.
• Chicken hackle feathers (dry-fly wings)
• Wing quill strips—duck, goose, and turkey
• Hairs
• Streamer hackle feathers
• Marabou

FLANK FEATHERS

These small to medium-size feathers are found on male ducks and certain female ducks along the sides of the body. The most notable is the famous barred wood duck feather, which the British call summer duck. Many classic patterns call for it, including the Quill Gordon, the Hendrickson, and the Light Cahill.

Other useful flank feathers include mallard and teal, which are easy to obtain, and widgeon, which is not. The characteristic all of these feathers share—along with a general similarity of shape—is the distinct barring, which gives them an attractive mottled appearance, like the wings of certain aquatic insects.

Flank feathers are used for both wet-fly and dry-fly wings. The dry-fly application is particularly common, with the elegant wood duck feather holding a legendary, almost mystical preference. It is a well-deserved one. The lemon-barred coloration is beautiful and insect-like, and the texture abets the formation of a neat and surprisingly durable pair of wings.

A material of great beauty, wood duck is costly and in short supply, even though the bird is once again plentiful on American flyways. The oriental mandarin is almost indistinguishable from our native bird, but is also expensive and not easily obtained. If you hunt, or have friends who do, perhaps you will have access to all the drake wood duck you can use. If not, dyed mallard or teal can be substituted. These feathers are not as lovely, but they are also not expensive. I particularly recommend them for the novice tyer.

CHICKEN HACKLE FEATHERS

Hackles refers to the feathers along the neck and shoulders of a bird. Many other types of feathers are used to put hackles on flies, but insofar as the term is applied to the bird's anatomy, we are referring to the neck/shoulder area.

We old country boys became hackle-conscious early in life. I used to look after my grandfather's chickens, and the roosters would flare their hackles when angry or threatened. After getting nailed a few times by their sharp spurs, I learned to give them a wide berth.

Fly-tying supply houses sell *necks* or *capes* of both roosters and hens. Mainly, the feathers are used to put hackles on flies, but some are also used for wings, and most attractive ones they can be, when proper selection is observed. The nice thing is that cheap hackles usually make much better wings than do the expensive ones used for hackling dry flies. Hen feathers, which have no value as dry-fly hackle whatever, are terrific for wings.

In some cases, a pair of feathers is used as-is, just as they come off the bird. For example, the popular Adams dry fly calls for two small feathers from the cape of barred rock, or Plymouth

Grizzly or barred rock cape (top) and saddle (bottom).

rock, chicken. Normally, we wouldn't reshape these feathers—they have just the right appearance.

In other cases, we may choose to alter the shape of a feather to improve the silhouette. Hen hackles usually require this. We either trim the feathers or use wing-formers.

WING QUILL STRIPS

Wings from waterfowl and certain game birds produce wonderful material for winging flies, wet flies in particular. Quills from both wild and domestic ducks and geese are commonly used, as are turkey wing quills. Among game birds, the woodcock has a particularly attractive feather of mottled brown. Woodcock cannot legally be offered for sale and must be obtained via hunting.

A great many aquatic insects have grey wings, and it is really an incredible piece of luck for fly-tyers that many ducks and geese do also. These are readily obtainable at moderate cost. Most duck quills are mallard, which is okay, but I do wish we could obtain black duck wings. Unfortunately, that magnificent species is on the decline, much to the concern of duck lovers.

The technique involved in making wings out of quill feathers is to cut a small section or strip from two corresponding feathers, one from a left wing and one from a right. These are tied to the hook in either the wet-fly or dry-fly style. Personally, I feel there are better materials for dry-fly wings, except on a few special patterns. But I use flight-feather strips extensively on wet flies.

HAIR

Various types of hair are used for constructing wings on dry flies, wet flies, and streamers. The list is a long one. Here are some of the most common:
- Deer tail, body, and facial hair
- Calf tail and body hair
- Squirrel tail
- Mink tail
- Fitch tail
- Fox guard hair
- Woodchuck tail and body hair
- Monga ringtails
- Skunk (don't laugh—it's great)

Of greatest interest to the typical fly-tyer, particularly the beginner, are calf and deer. A tremendous variety of wings may be tied using the body, facial, and tail hairs from these two creatures.

Deer tails, or *bucktails,* as they are commonly called, are used primarily for tying streamers. The natural coloration is white and mottled brown, both of which are called for on many patterns. Also, bucktails are dyed practically every color imaginable.

Bucktails have significant differences owing to the age, size, and species of the deer. Generally I opt for medium- to large-size bucktails with long, straight hairs. For very small streamers, small tails with fine hairs are better. Some species of deer have crinkly tail hairs, and I don't get my best results with those.

Deer body hair ranges from white to tan to grey to mottled grey-brown. The length and texture also varies greatly, depending on the part of the pelt from which the hair is taken and the species of deer. Climate and time of year also influence the properties of deer hair.

The two major applications of deer body hair are for dry-fly wings and for trimmed hair bodies. Interestingly, we look for dramatically different characteristics when selecting hair for these two applications. For wings, we want fine-textured hair that has minimal tendency to crimp or flare. For bodies, we look for thicker hair that flares readily when thread pressure is applied. Both of these types are available commercially. It is important to tell your dealer what the hair will be used for when making a purchase.

An excellent hair for wings may be obtained from a deer's face, or mask. This hair does not crimp at all, and it is about the right length and consistency for constructing dry-fly wings. The coloration runs to grey-brown, which matches the shading of various stream insects quite well.

Calf tails come in natural shades of brown, black, and white, but they are also dyed a multitude of colors. The longer hairs make pretty fair streamers, provided they are not too crinkly or twisted. The shorter hairs that are found near the butt end are very good for dry-fly wings. The famous Wulff series of dry flies may be winged with calf tail hair. This hair tends to be rather hard and slippery, not the easiest material with which to work. A modicum of skill is required before tackling the calf-tail wing, which is why the Royal Wulff pattern lesson comes late in the book.

Calf body hair is my preference for dry-fly wings. It is finer, softer, and easier to work with than tail hair. While rather short, the hair length is adequate for all but the largest fly sizes. I am pleased to find that calf body hair is now obtainable from better materials houses; it was a difficult item to come by for many years.

To attempt to analyze the many types of hair used in fly-tying would, I believe, tend to complicate a beginner's book. Suffice to say that the tyer is at liberty to substitute one for the other, where the appearance, texture, and behavioral characteristics are similar. For example, black squirrel or skunk makes an excellent substitute for black bucktail. When dressing hairwing salmon flies, I often substitute woodchuck for the hard-to-obtain grey fox. These are things one learns during the course of a fly-tying career.

I should mention that artificial hairs are now available, some of which can be used to pleasing effect. FisHair—that's a brand name, not generic—is a marvelous creation. It comes in many colors and has a brilliance and translucence similar to polar bear hair. It is available in six-inch or ten-inch lengths, the latter favored by the saltwater fly-tying contingent.

I have found another excellent synthetic in hobby shops. Called craft fur, it is used for various handcrafts, particularly as hair for dolls and little animals. It is the easiest and most manageable material I have ever used, as it compresses under thread pressure, thus causing the least amount of bulk. It is color-fast and very "alive" in the water. We will utilize this material in one of the streamer-fly pattern lessons.

STREAMER HACKLE FEATHERS

Larger feathers from rooster capes and saddles make attractive wings on streamer flies. As we have learned, streamers don't imitate insects—they imitate baitfish. Why, therefore, is one of the main components referred to as the "wings" of a streamer? Simply because that's what someone originally chose to name it, and no one has come up with anything better, including me.

Actually, these feathers represent the shape or outline of a fish. In patterns designed to simulate a particular baitfish, feather coloration and markings are chosen with a close match in mind. Carrie Stevens' Grey Ghost pattern is a prime example—the olive-grey feathers specified in the dressing are intended to simulate the color of a freshwater smelt that abound in the lakes of Maine.

Quite a number of streamer patterns employ feathers with black center stripes to imitate the several striped minnows that are found in trout waters. The most notable of these is the Black-Nosed Dace, which has a pronounced black stripe down the side. These minnows, once ubiquitous, are now found in only those streams which have somehow escaped pollution and degradation. They are more environmentally sensitive than some trout.

MARABOU

According to an old George Leonard Herter catalog, marabou (sometimes spelled: maribou) originally came from a stork. This *may* be true. I do know that babies don't come from storks, stork chicks excluded. Charming as those old Herter's catalogs were, the credibility gaps were sometimes alarming.

Today's marabou comes from white domestic turkeys. Dry, marabou looks like a bunch of fluff—which indeed it is. Wet, it slims out into a fish-like form and is very active in the water. This property makes marabou a superb material for streamer-fly wings.

Marabou is inexpensive and is available in a great array of colors, including natural white. Of the various streamer-wing materials, it is the easiest to apply.

DRY-FLY HACKLE MATERIALS

There is a little confusion and a great mystique surrounding the subject of hackle. In part, this has to do with the term itself. In the section on wing materials, I used the word in a narrow frame of reference to describe certain feathers on a chicken. Ultimately, hackles can be any feather or, for that matter, any material used to create that particular component of a fly which is called the hackle.

Much has been written about hackle. In *Mastering the Art of Fly-Tying,* I devoted a major chapter to the subject. That was for the edification of the intermediate-level tyer. Here, we will discuss hackle at the introductory level, with more specifics included in the pattern lessons.

The hackle on a dry fly serves three main purposes:
• Coloration
• Floatation
• Silhouette

As to coloration, the idea is to create a light pattern which is attractive to the fish. In many cases, this implies matching or simulating the coloration of a natural insect. Fortunately for us, fish see these insects through water, and therefore, imperfectly. If trout could see insects as we do, without the reflective and refractive effects of water, we would rarely fool them. I think this may be why birds which pick insects off the water seldom make a mistake and seize an angler's imitation.

One of the predominant features on an insect is its wings. We have learned that wing coloration makes a major contribution to the light pattern a trout sees, more so than the tiny feet which touch the water. So, a major consideration in imitative fly-tying is the matching of hackle color to the wings of the insect we are attempting to simulate.

With common stream insects—mayflies in particular—greys tend to predominate. These range from the palest off-white to almost-black. This accounts for the great popularity of grey hackle. In fly-tyer's jargon, grey is generally referred to as *dun,* a British term which has stayed with us.

In books and fly-tying catalogs, you will see *dun* used in combination with various other terms, in order to more accurately describe a particular shade. Here are a few of the more common ones:
• Dun—medium grey
• Dark dun—dark grey
• Pale watery dun—very light grey
• Sandy dun—grey with a bronze cast

- Rusty dun—grey with a distinct rusty cast
- Honey dun—grey with a cream or ginger cast

Duns are a product of crossbreeding. Even with today's accumulated data base in genetic engineering, this is an imperfect process. There are great variations in the birds bred for fly-tying and hackles must be checked for certain undesirable aberrations, not only in color, but in the quality of the feathers themselves. Some have stiff, overly thick center quills that cause the feather to twist and roll when being wound onto the hook. Others have hooked or curved barbules which behave poorly during the winding process. These are to be avoided when selecting capes.

Some other important natural hackle shades are:
- Cream—a delicate off-white shade
- Straw cream—slightly darker, straw-like
- Ginger—darker still
- Brown—dark ginger color
- Coachman brown—dark, rich brown, almost chocolate

These colors are specified for many popular fly patterns. Gingers and browns are fairly common, as these are the natural shades of certain breeds of chicken. Creams and coachman browns are more scarce but obtainable.

Another extremely important shade is actually more of a pattern than a color. I refer to it as barred rock or Plymouth rock, but it is most commonly called grizzly. That's another old British term. Originally, it was grizzle, which perhaps was too unappetizing for we aesthetes of angling, hence the modification.

Barred rock, or grizzly hackle, is composed of white and black barrings. It lends a distinctive mottled or diffused effect to a fly, and is commonly used in combination with other colors to produce a more life-like shading. I am very partial to it.

Sometimes barred rocks are crossbred to produce hackle that has the characteristics of both breeds. We see such shades as barred ginger, dun grizzly, and cree. These are the marked capes that I favor—particularly the cree, which is a mix of various browns, gingers, greys, and black. Good cree necks are a genetic accident and are not plentiful, so when I see a quality cape, I snap it up.

Crossbreeding produces other aberrations in shading. Splashed capes are quite common, particularly in the duns. These capes have feathers that vary in shade from one to the other or are tinged with a shade other than the base color. Some interesting effects can also be obtained by using hackles with these characteristics.

There are a few other combination shades that are fairly common and are called for on certain useful patterns. Two which appear in most catalogs are:
- Badger—White, cream, or ginger with a black center
- Furnace—Dark ginger or brown with a black center

Some very attractive effects are obtained via the use of badger and furnace as dry-fly hackles. In addition, these feathers are incorporated in some excellent streamer-fly dressings.

Sometimes, capes are dyed to produce a desired color. I have no problem with this provided it is properly done. The most common problem is that the temperature of the dye bath is too hot; this cooks the fibres and stems, ruining the quality. Also, the skin of dyed capes tends to be brittle, so care must be taken when handling them lest they break into pieces.

There is a cold-dye process used to produce various shades of dun which has become quite popular. I refer to photo-dyeing. The capes are soaked in a silver nitrate solution and then run through a regular black-and-white film developing sequence. The shading is controlled by timing and by the natural color of the feathers. The results can be beautiful.

While my preference is for naturally colored feathers, I don't concur with the widely held opinion that dyed hackles are to be shunned. I believe modern expertise in dying techniques can produce a most acceptable result. For many years I used dyed hackles because I couldn't find or afford naturals, dun in particular. My flies looked good, and I caught tons of fish. The main consideration, besides the dying process, is the quality of the cape itself.

What constitutes quality? As we learned in *Zen and the Art of Motorcycle Maintenance,* quality cannot be defined in the abstract—it must be applied to something. In the case of dry-fly hackle, there are some tangible points of quality which we look for when selecting hackle.

There is a correlation between our second major dry-fly attribute, floatation and hackle quality. Hackle is instrumental in causing a fly to float, more so in some designs than others. With classic dry flies, we want a high-riding float, and so we seek hackles which will abet this. We also want feathers which are manageable, wrap neatly, and are true to size. Thus, the main quality points we look for when selecting capes are:

• Stiffness and liveliness of barbules or fibres
• Fineness and flexibility of center quill
• Trueness and consistency of length of fibres when flared ninety degrees from the quill
• Freedom from excessive web in the prime area

In addition to feather quality, there are several other considerations which should be taken into account when selecting a cape. They have to do with practicality and economics:

• Amount of usable hackle on the cape
• Size of usable hackles
• Presence of feathers which suit other applications

Top-quality (left) and poor-quality (right) hackle feathers. Note relative absence of web and uniformity of barbule length in good feather.

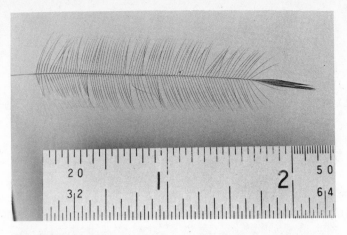

Better-grade dry-fly hackles have
excellent "useable-length" characteristics.

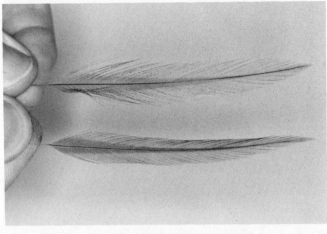

These two feathers appear reasonably
similar until flexed; then the
better quality feather on the right is
seen to have more barbule density
along the quill and is more true to size,
in terms of barbule length.

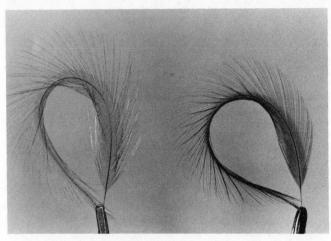

A throat hackle. Note long, stiff
barbules near tip.

The amount of usable hackle is a clear enough consideration—the more hackles, the more desirable the cape. However, we must consider hackle size also and perhaps alternative uses for the hackle as well. Let's look at a few examples.

Suppose you want to purchase a dun cape for tying standard dry flies in sizes 12 and 14 and perhaps a few size 16s. You don't care about smaller flies. Therefore, all you need be concerned with is the quality and quantity of size 12, 14, and 16 hackles on a cape. This simplifies the process and may allow you to obtain a suitable cape for less than top dollar, because:

- Capes with a generous quantity of medium-sized hackles are more common than those which also have a lot of feathers in a wider range of sizes, especially smaller sizes.
- Range of hackle size is a prime consideration applied by the dealer when grading capes. Thus, a cape which will tie a wide range of sizes will generally cost more.

Let's take another case. You want to tie all the way down to size 22, and also dress a few large, variant-type flies. Now you must search for a truly prime cape and pay the going price, or you must buy two capes.

Now let's bring item 3 into the decision-making process. By "other applications," I mean, in this case, uses besides the hackling of medium-sized dry flies. For instance, are there plenty of wide feathers along the sides of the cape with long, stiff barbules? This is great tailing material, and that's worth something. And suppose the cape has lots of big feathers that are nicely shaped for making streamer wings. For the person who wants to fish a Grey Ghost between hatches, that's added value.

I could go on and on. The point is simply that utility, as well as quality, should be considered when selecting capes.

Silhouette, the third major dry-fly attribute, is more a matter of pattern and technique than hackle procurement, but there is some relationship. In one of the pattern lessons we will tie the Dun Variant, which depends upon its silhouette for its effectiveness to a large extent. This is a big dry fly which calls for oversize hackles. Capes which have decent-quality large hackles will probably have no small ones to speak of.

Since we are on the subject of large hackles, this is an appropriate time to mention *saddle hackles*. The saddle is that area below the cape, in other words, the mid-portion of the bird's back. These hackles may or may not be suitable for dry-fly work—one must apply the same criteria as when grading a cape. When quality is there, saddle hackles make superb large dry flies and cost much less than cape hackles of comparable quality.

Be particularly cautious when judging saddles, as they tend to look much better than they actually are. Watch out for overly thick stems. Flex the feather into a simulation of the wrapped position and check the barbule length. See if the feather tends to twist or roll.

When purchasing capes, you will have a choice between domestics raised expressly for fly-tying, and imported birds grown primarily for eggs and meat. Despite the fact that the imported birds are not bred for hackles and seldom live long enough to become prime, they are sometimes of remarkably good quality. These capes are much cheaper than the domestics, and a good one can be quite a bargain.

Don't misread that last statement. The so-called genetic capes benefit from scientific methods and strict supervision and are usually superior to even the best imports. The one area (besides price) where imports sometimes have an advantage is the presence of decent-quality large hackles. The reason is that domestic hackle-growers breed for quality and quantity in the smaller size ranges, which is mainly what the market calls for.

There was a time when dry-fly capes of great size were imported from China. They had no small hackles, but quite often the large feathers were excellent. I have a few hidden away which don't tie smaller than a size 12, but oh, those Variants! I have not been able to obtain dry-fly-quality Chinese capes for some time.

I mention the Chinese capes not for nostalgic reasons, but because one never knows what might happen there. At this writing, China is on a "capitalistic" cycle, and relations with the United States are quite good. It wouldn't shock me if they were to start exporting dry-fly capes again in quantity, given the dramatic growth of the fly-tying market. It also wouldn't surprise me if other emerging countries did likewise. One can always hope.

WET-FLY HACKLE MATERIALS

For purposes of this discussion, let us consider any fly designed to be fished below the surface a wet fly. This includes classic-style wet flies, soft-hackle wet flies, nymphs, and even certain streamers. While feathers from various birds are used to hackle these flies, there is a common quality which allows such a grouping.

The quality to which I refer is that of action, or behavior. With subaqueous flies, movement is an important attribute. It is desirable that the hackles are sufficiently soft and absorbent that they will undulate enticingly when fished. I consider this to be of at least equal importance to color and shading.

The following is a list of feathers commonly used as wet-fly hackle:
- Soft rooster or hen, from capes or saddles
- Grouse/partridge
- Hen pheasant
- Mallard/teal flank
- Guinea fowl
- Woodcock
- Speckled hen saddles

While these feathers may vary widely in coloration, markings, and other characteristics, they all have that soft quality which allows them to come alive under water. Flies dressed in this manner can be deadly, especially when the angler has gained a modicum of skill in their use.

This completes our basic orientation in materials. There is an awesome variety of stuff being tied to hooks today, with more innovation, invention, and discovery going on constantly. Hopefully, this chapter has started the student in a good direction by creating an understanding of the attributes of the more important materials.

There is one more item I wish to cover in this chapter, even though it isn't a material, per se. I refer to the cement or lacquer used to coat the heads of flies, and also for certain other operations. The functions of head cement are:
- To secure the head of the fly and protect the thread under actual fishing conditions
- To strengthen, protect, and lock in place certain materials and components during the tying process
- To contribute to the aesthetics of the fly by effecting an attractive finished appearance

Head cements seem to come and go in the marketplace. I've tried quite a few, some of which I liked and some of which I did not. At this writing, I am using Price's head cement and am pleased with it because it performs all three functions quite well. It is also quick-drying, another desirable attribute.

Head cement should be maintained at a certain consistency, which requires that the tyer have a supply of thinner on hand. If the cement becomes too thick, it will not penetrate well. If it becomes too thin, it penetrates too much and doesn't produce a good-looking protective coating. Dealers usually carry thinners for the cements they sell. These are common solvents, such as toluol, acetone, and methyl ethyl ketone. Thinner should be added in small amounts until the desired consistency is obtained.

Be extremely careful with thinners—they are usually quite flammable and rather noxious. Use them in a well-ventilated room, and avoid breathing the fumes. I've had several unpleasant experiences due to inhaling more of that stuff than was good for me.

6

THREAD MANAGEMENT

Fly-tying begins and ends with thread managemet, literally. The first move is to tie onto the hook, the final one to tie off. In between, virtually every operation is disciplined by thread management. It is the very essence of fly-tying. Given its importance, let's begin our hands-on exercises with an examination of the essential thread-management techniques.

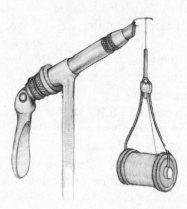

TYING ON

This one is easy—it is simply a matter of wrapping the thread over itself on the hook shank, so that it is maintained there by the weight of the bobbin.

Before we do an actual tie-on, let's load the thread into a bobbin and adjust the tension. First, mount the spool in the bobbin, as shown. Then, run the wire loop of your bobbin-threader through the tube toward the spool of thread.

Pull off about six inches of thread, and run it through the loop of the threader. Now just pull the loop back through the tube, and your bobbin is threaded.

It is important to maintain a level of tension on the thread so that it can be pulled readily from the spool without danger of breakage but will not feed out merely from the weight of the bobbin. I find most new bobbins are too tight. The tension may be reduced by gently bending the limbs outward, but this must be done carefully, lest the bobbin be damaged. Don't just spread the

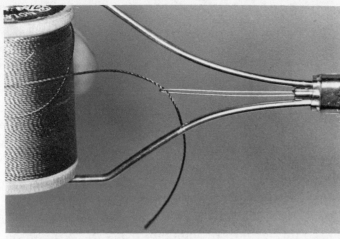

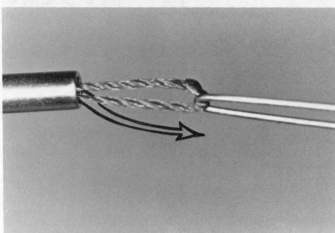

Loading the bobbin.

limbs, as though you were doing the old wishbone routine, or you may get the same result. Work on each limb individually, and progress very gradually. If you don't feel quite secure with this, get an experienced tyer to assist you.

Now for the tie-on.

1. Mount a hook in the vise, per the illustration in Chapter 2. Then take the thread coming out of the bobbin tube with the left thumb and forefinger while holding the bobbin in the right hand. A note to left-handed people: simply reverse all instructions, and you will have no problems—or at least, no more problems than the rest of us.

2. Position the thread so that it is underneath the hook shank and at a right angle to it.

The starting position—thread behind hook.

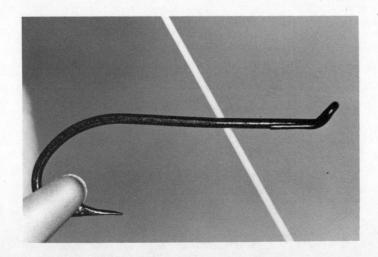

3. With the bobbin hand, bring the thread upward against the hook and take a turn around the shank. *Always wind away from yourself.* In other words, if you were facing the eye of the hook, the movement would be clockwise.

4. Now take another turn, this time working toward the rear, so that the thread crosses over itself.

5. Take perhaps a half-dozen more turns, working back toward the bend. Hold the bobbin in a horizontal position, and work fairly close to the hook shank, as illustrated.

6. Let go of the bobbin. You will see that it hangs suspended below the hook. Hold the tag end of thread with the left hand, and cut the thread off flush with the hook, using a scissor-blade like a lance. Be sure not to nick any of the turns of thread you have made around the hook.

That's all there is to tying on. As we shall see further on, we sometimes vary the position on the hook at which we tie on, in order to set up properly for the particular tying process. Also, we may use contiguous wraps or spaced wraps in various cases, as dictated by the situation.

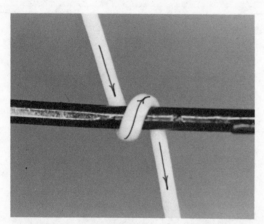

The first turn is toward the eye.

Wrap the thread back over itself.

Thread is secured to hook shank.

TYING OFF

That's right, we haven't even tied a fly, and here we are learning to tie off. I strongly suggest you practice this technique on a bare hook until a modicum of competence is achieved. Thus you may save your very first fly without wrecking it by fumbling the final step.

Tying off is done by making a whip-finish around the very front of the hook. It's a bit more involved than tying on, but once learned it becomes easy, and like swimming or bike riding, it is never forgotten.

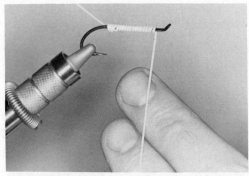

The starting position—right index and middle finger behind thread with finger-nails facing you.

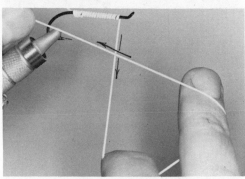

Form loop by hooking thread around middle finger. Thread that forms loop is in front of thread coming from hook.

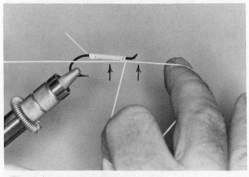

Use middle finger to position thread against throat of hook.

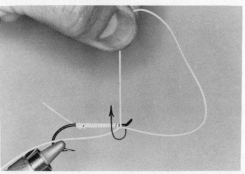

Use left hand to make first pass around hook. If necessary, use right hand to keep thread properly positioned, as shown.

What actually happens during the whip-finish is that a noose is formed around the neck of the fly immediately behind the eye of the hook. The noose is then tightened by pulling on the thread while holding the noose taut with a bodkin. The illustrations and captions define the various steps in the whip-finish procedure.

The tie-on and the whip-finish are thread-handling processes which do not involve any other materials—they simply have to do with the thread and the hook. Now let us examine three important techniques that are required for affixing materials to the hook throughout the tying progression and for deploying them in the desired manner.

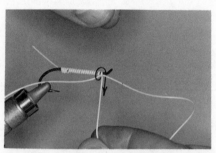

Catch thread with right hand as it comes under the hook.

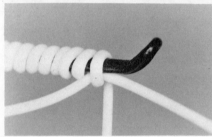

At this point, here is how the whip finish in progress should appear.

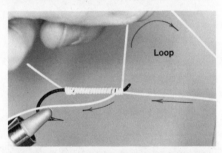

Five wraps is considered optimal (only three shown here, due to bulk of demonstration material). Try to work in forward direction. Catch loop with scissors tip or bodkin and tighten noose by pulling on the loose end of the thread.

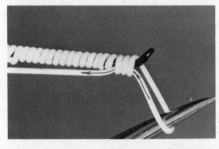

Completed whip finish.

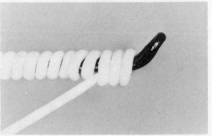

THE PINCH

I believe the pinch to be the single most important technique in successful fly-tying. It is used to attach and secure materials precisely in the position in which they are mounted on the hook. In other words, the pinch fastens materials where the tyer's fingers place them.

The pinch is quite easy to execute, as the pictures and captions illustrate. In this exercise, we see a small bunch of fibres from a mallard duck flank feather being positioned and fastened to the top of the hook. This is the manner in which materials of this type are affixed preparatory to forming the popular wood-duck wing, which is employed in such patterns as the Quill Gordon, the Hendrickson, and the Light Cahill. Note that we have neatly applied a layer of thread to that portion of the hook shank where the fibres are to be tied in. There are very few procedures that call for materials to be tied to a bare hook shank.

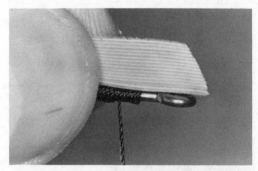

Position material precisely where it is to be tied on—in this case, atop the hook.

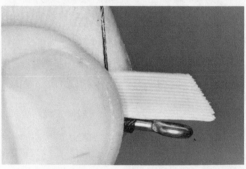

Bring thread straight upward on near side of material, catching it between left thumb and forefinger.

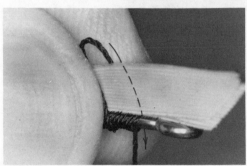

While maintaining thread/material positioning with pinch, bring thread over material and down behind the hook.

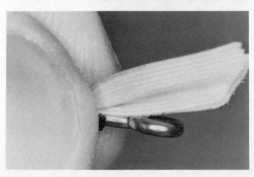

Left: Tie material in place with downward pull on thread while maintaining pinch.

Right: Repeat once or twice to secure the material in place.

THE DISTRIBUTION WRAP

This technique is also quite simple, and is second in importance only to the pinch. It is used to affix materials to a hook while at the same time causing them to be deployed or flared partially around the hook. In the exercise, the pictures and captions show how the distribution wrap is utilized to apply legs or soft hackles, as would be done with a nymph or subsurface fly.

Early in your fly-tying career you will learn that there are subtle variations of the distribution wrap which are employed to create desired effects. These will be studied in the pattern lessons further on.

Position the material on the far side of the hook, then begin first wrap.
Notice that the material is not pinched between the left thumb and forefinger.

Allow the material to be deployed by the thread. As the wrap progresses, you may wish to help the material deploy itself with discrete manipulations of the left forefinger and thumb.

Bring the thread upward, securing the material in the manner shown, or as desired.

The result.

THE SLACK LOOP

This technique is a bit more difficult than the distribution wrap but not prohibitively so. In actuality, it is an extension of the distribution wrap. It is used to cause materials to distribute or flare completely and evenly around a hook.

The most common use of the slack loop is in the affixing of deer hair to a hook shank. The hair will subsequently be trimmed to form a buoyant body or the head of the ever-popular Muddler Minnow. I have chosen not to include the clipped-hair process in this book, as I consider it to be at least an intermediate-level technique. To demonstrate the slack loop, I have illustrated the deployment of hackle fibers around the entire circumference of a hook. This is an important alternative to winding a hackle because many hackle feathers do not lend themselves to the winding or wrapping process.

These thread-management techniques, with a few variations, will enable you to tie practically any fly, even the most complex and sophisticated. As you go along, you will adapt them to your own style and personal methodology. The following pattern lessons will provide ample opportunity to practice and master thread management.

Start is similar to distribution wrap. At this point, there is no tension on the thread; it is simply touching the material.

Form 1½ loops before beginning to apply tension to thread. Material should be evenly deployed, and should completely encircle the hook. Assist with fingers as required, and continue wrapping while increasing thread tension.

The result.

DISASTER-AVERSION TECHNIQUE:
WHAT TO DO IF THE THREAD BREAKS.

Inevitably, thread will break during tying. Sometimes this is the tyer's fault, sometimes it is due to the inconsistencies of thread quality. In either case, the idea is to save the fly. Here's how:

1. When a thread break occurs, immediately seize the end dangling from the hook and restore tension.

2. Grip the broken end with your hackle pliers and let their weight maintain tension while you tie on again.

3. Take several firm wraps behind the hackle pliers, securing the broken end.

4. Make whatever repairs are necessary, and proceed with the fly.

Thanks to the memory inherent in pre-waxed thread, this technique works much of the time. Each case must be dealt with individually in terms of what must be done to restore the partially completed fly to the point reached prior to the thread break.

7

THE BASIC BLACK

TECHNIQUES TO BE LEARNED

1. Yarn-wrapped body
2. Winding hackle

Let's begin with about as easy a pattern as one might encounter, a soft-hackle wet fly consisting of only a body and hackle. I call this pattern the Basic Black. As your wife or lady friend will attest, basic black is simple but devastatingly effective.

PATTERN DESCRIPTION

HOOK: Standard wet fly, size 10
THREAD: Black, standard pre-waxed
BODY: Black yarn
HACKLE: Black feather

TYING STEPS

1. Mount the hook in the vise.

2. Tie on, starting the thread approximately twenty percent of the shank length back from the eye of the hook.

3. Wind the thread in even, contiguous wraps nearly but not quite back to the bend of the hook. At some point during this process, trim off the excess tag end.

4. Select a piece of average-thickness yarn about three inches (75 mm) in length.

5. Trim the yarn on an angle, so it will taper nicely when wrapped onto the hook with the thread. A straight cut will result in a bump in the underbody.

6. With the left thumb and forefinger, hold the yarn on top of the hook at the bend. Position the yarn so that the taper-cut end extends approximately to where the thread was tied on.

7. Tie the yarn to the hook shank using the pinch technique illustrated in the previous chapter.

8. Bind down the yarn which lies along the hook shank by working forward with contiguous wraps of thread under moderately firm tension.

9. Proceed to a position two or three wraps of thread beyond the tie-in point. Compare your fly to that in the corresponding illustration. It should be reasonably similar.

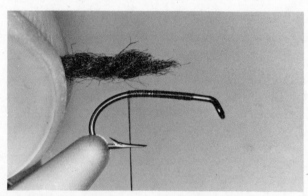

The starting position, with thread wrapped nearly to bend. Note how hook is mounted in vise. Also note yarn, taper-trimmed, in tie-on position.

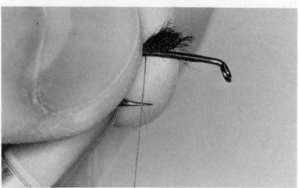

Use pinch to tie on yarn.

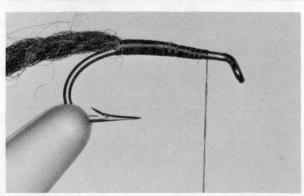

Wrap thread forward to this point.

10. Now begin to wrap the yarn around the hook, progressing forward, with each wrap snug against the previous one, so as to form a smooth, tight body. This is a two-handed procedure: you pass the yarn over with the left hand and catch it coming under with the right. Note that on the first wrap, the yarn will want to slide slightly behind the tie-in point—not all of it, but perhaps a half or third of the skein. This is good because it helps avoid creating a bump at that point and contributes to the formation of a nice taper. This is why I instructed you to tie in the yarn just slightly ahead of the beginning of the bend.

11. When you reach the point where the thread is hanging, bind the yarn to the underside of the hook. This is done by holding the yarn with the right hand and passing the bobbin over the hook with the left hand. Use firm wraps, but take care not to break the thread. The weight of the bobbin is sufficient to maintain tension so that you can let go of it after making the wrap and then catch it coming underneath. This is all done with the left hand, while the right hand holds the yarn. Three or four wraps should suffice.

12. Now we must trim off the excess yarn. Here, I want you to learn two neat little tricks which will soon become automatic:

   A. While holding the yarn taut with the left thumb and forefinger, use the middle finger to catch the thread and hold it back out of the way.

   B. When you trim the yarn, trim it close to the tie-down point, but not right up against the thread. In other words, leave a very tiny tag end. This facilitates two things: the yarn can be further secured with a few more turns of thread, and a smoother surface will be created over which to wrap the hackle.

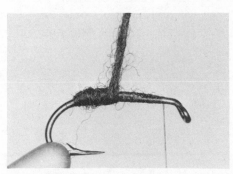

Wrapping the yarn.

Yarn being secured with thread.

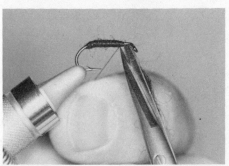

Cutting off excess yarn. Note how fingers are used to keep thread away from scissors blades.

13. This is not so much a tying step as an admonition: from this point on, be especially conscious of spacing. Do not crowd the eye of the hook—you still have a hackle to affix, and you will need room for the whip-finish. Examine the illustrations carefully before proceeding.

14. Take a few turns of thread forward to bind down that tiny tag of yarn, then a few more turns back to the front of the body. Be very neat here. If you notice any little bumps or crevices, try to smooth them out with a discreet wrap of thread, but don't build up any bulk. I know that sounds a bit contradictory, but after a few practice flies, you will see how it works.

15. Select a hackle feather from a black hen or soft rooster cape. For standard soft-hackle wet flies, I usually use slightly longer fibres than I would on a comparable-size dry fly. This means that when stroked to stand out at a right angle from the stem of the feather, the barbules will be approximately twice the gape of the hook.

16. Carefully strip off the waste material toward the butt end of the feather, one side at a time.

17. Bind the stem to the bottom of the hook shank at the front end of the yarn body. Simply hold the feather with the left hand at approximately a forty-five-degree attitude, with the tiniest bit of stem showing. You may find it helpful to sneak the first wrap of thread around the stem and hook under very slight tension, so as to keep the stem from being pushed around the hook shank. Then secure with five or six snug, contiguous wraps. Again, I implore you: don't crowd the eye.

18. Trim off the excess stem in the same manner you did the yarn, cutting on a bias, if possible. It is helpful on a turned-down-eye hook to do your trimming slightly off to the side, rather than directly underneath, in the throat area. This helps keep the hook eye clear.

19. Take another two or three turns of thread to bury and further secure the stem.

20. Now we shall wind the hackle in the simple, straight forward manner we would on a dry fly. Seize the tip of the feather with the hackle pliers: be sure to include the stem, or center quill.

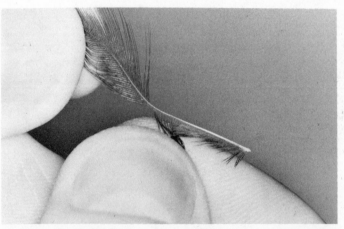

A soft-fibred hackle.
Strip off excess material.

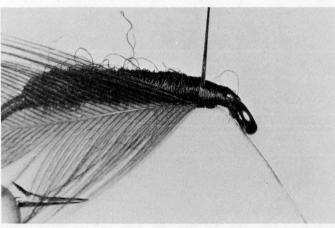

Tie in stem beneath hook shank.
After stem is secured, clip off
excess quill.

You may seize it straight on or at a slight angle, as it suits you. Then simply wind the hackle over and around the hook under gentle tension, taking care not to break the stem. This is a two-handed procedure, similar to the wrapping of the yarn: over with the left hand, catch the pliers coming under the hook with the right hand.

21. On this fly, you will only need two or perhaps three turns, depending on the density and fibrosity of the hackle. The turns should be contiguous, stem against stem. Do not let barbules from the previous turn be bound down or flared forward by the turn in progress—stroke them back with the left hand if necessary.

22. When sufficient turns of hackle have been made, let the remaining feather hang suspended from the hook, with tension maintained by the weight of the hackle pliers. Wrap the thread around the hook and stem immediately forward of the hackle, binding the stem to the underside of the hook. The idea is to work the thread against the stem without catching any of the excess barbules—or at least, as few as possible. Use your left hand to reach over the hook and hold the hackle pliers, so that the stem and extraneous barbules are not driven into the throat area by the tension of the thread. Three or four very firm wraps should suffice.

23. Protect the thread as learned earlier and trim off the stem and excess material using the very tips of the scissors. Then bind down and further secure the end of the stem with a few more tight wraps.

Beginning position for winding hackle.

Hackle-winding in progress.

At this point, secure the hackle with thread wraps while holding excess clear of the eye with the hackle pliers. Clip off excess, taking care to avoid cutting thread.

24. Execute the whip-finish, and you have completed your first fly. If you are afraid you might blow the whip-finish, make three tight half-hitches and either do the whip-finish over them (fail-safe approach) or stop right there and apply an extra coat of head cement.

25. Apply head cement with a needle, toothpick, or very slim brush. Don't let it run into the hackle, and by all means, keep it out of the hook eye. Should you inadvertently fill the eye with cement, run a small waste feather through it right away, before the cement dries. Let the first coat dry completely, then apply a second. If you tied off with half-hitches, apply a third coating.

Whip finish.

The completed fly.

Applying head cement.

DISASTER-AVERSION TECHNIQUE: WHAT TO DO WHEN THE WHIP-FINISH GOES AWRY.

Now and then you will lose a whip-finish, and this will never cease entirely—it still happens to me. Most often, it won't be your fault—it will be due to the thread being frayed, so that when you attempt to pull the noose tight, a bump of balled-up fibres develops which won't slip through the overwraps. Here's what to do:

1. If you know ahead of time that the thread is frayed, finish off with half-hitches.

2. If the condition is moderate and the ball-up is very small, let the thread tension relax so that the little glitch may pass beneath the overwraps. Then tighten.

3. If the loop is large enough, you can undo the overwraps and start the whip-finish over, using a smaller loop, so that the thread ball is already beyond the overwraps.

4. If you can't execute #3, undo the overwraps anyway and apply half-hitches.

A few additional notes about yarn here would be useful. As mentioned in the materials chapter, there is a tremendous proliferation of yarns available today in terms of material, thickness, texture, color, and other properties. I often see yarns in fabric or knitting shops which are just super for fly-tying. Some have gorgeous, tweedy mottlings, very attractive and very insect-like.

Don't hesitate to experiment. Use whatever looks good to you. And don't be put off if the thickness isn't what you want—you can easily separate the strands to reduce bulk or double up to increase it.

Incidentally, the Golden Darter pattern lesson will teach you how to make a floss body by starting near the front, wrapping back to the bend, then forward again. You can also do this with fine-denier yarns. The Fur-Bodied Soft-Hackle lesson teaches a technique called *teasing,* whereby the body is rendered fuzzier for enhanced translucence. You can do that to a wool body also, should you so desire.

8

THE OLIVE/GROUSE
SOFT-HACKLE

TECHNIQUES TO BE LEARNED

1. Dubbed body, using single-thread technique
2. Use of grouse and similar feathers for hackle

This soft-hackle fly is somewhat similar to the Basic Black, but uses different materials and, therefore, somewhat different methodology. The simple, single-thread dubbing technique is appropriate for softer, more workable materials which tend to spin onto the thread easily. I like it for the more petite flies, where the spinning-loop method may contribute too much bulk. Most of my dubbed-body dry flies are dressed using the single-thread technique.

Incidently, while the pattern description calls for olive, feel free to substitute another color, so long as the type of material is the same. Olive is very effective at times, but so are other colors. We are concerned with methodology here, not precise shade.

PATTERN DESCRIPTION

HOOK: Standard wet fly, size 10
THREAD: Olive or white, pre-waxed
BODY: Olive dubbing, synthetic or fur, smooth and soft
HACKLE: Brown/grey mottled grouse or partridge feather

TYING STEPS

1. Mount the hook and tie on near the front, approximately twenty percent of the shank length behind the eye. Wrap to within two turns of where the bend begins to slope off.
2. Expose about three inches (75 mm) of thread and apply a thin coating of wax.

60

3. Spin the dubbing onto the thread, a little at a time, forming an attractive taper. About two inches (50 mm) of material will suffice. Strive for neatness and smoothness, adding or deleting small quantities of materials to compensate for bumps and gaps. Try to work the dubbing in a clockwise direction, so that when you wrap it around the hook it will not untwist. This is even more critical with coarse materials.

NOTE: It is difficult to dub right up against the hook shank. This is why we stopped the thread two turns shy of the bend. The short length of bare thread between the upper extremity of the dubbing and the hook will be used up in the next step.

4. Make two turns to the rear. The thread should now be at the bend, and the dubbing in contact with the hook, so that with the next wrap, dubbing is deployed around the hook shank.

5. Wrap the dubbing around the hook, working forward, with neat, contiguous turns. If the dubbing remaining on the thread appears to loosen during this procedure, re-spin, using the right thumb and forefinger.

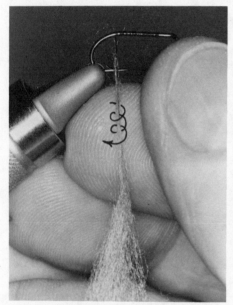

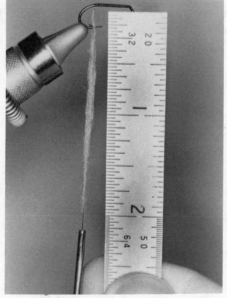

Left: Spinning the dubbing onto the thread.

Right: Measuring for proper proportions.

Where the dubbed body begins.

Wrapping the dubbing.

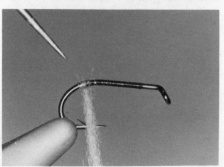

6. As you approach the original tie-in point, try to estimate whether or not the material remaining is just the right amount to complete the body. If more is needed, add a small wisp. If it appears there is a bit too much—one turn of extra dubbing, let us say—pack it tighter and try to get it to fit. Allow a small but sufficient amount of space for the hackle and head, as shown in the photograph.

NOTE: With soft dubbing materials, it is allowable to wrap back over the front part of the body, then forward again, in order to develop the desired shaping. This takes a little practice. The effect will vary with the properties of the material.

7. Select a grouse or partridge feather which resembles the one in the illustration. The hackle-size criteria, or barbule length, is the same as specified for the Basic Black. Grouse hackle is very dense and webby, so you won't need much, two turns at most. Prepare the feather as follows:

    A. Strip off the waste fibres in the butt area.

    B. Gently stroke the barbules back so that they stand out at right angles to the center quill on either side.

    C. Trim off the barbules at the tip end, so that approximately ³⁄₁₆ inches (5 mm) of hackle material remains, measured along the center quill.

8. Tie in the hackle beneath the shank, by the *tip end*.

9. Seize the *butt end* of the center quill with the hackle pliers and wrap the hackle. Be very careful with tension—grouse feathers have delicate quills. As you wind, try to stroke back the barbules so that they all lie behind the center quill and slant slightly rearward. One and one-half to two turns of hackle is sufficient.

10. Tie down and trim off excess quill; be careful to avoid cutting the thread. Whip-finish and cement.

The completed body and the hackle feather.

Hackle feather prepared for tie-in.

Hackle feather is tied in at throat beneath hook, by the tip.

Winding grouse hackle. As you wind, stroke fibers rearward.

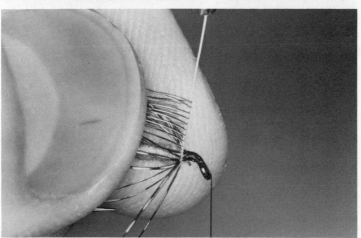

One to two turns of grouse hackle is sufficient. Trim as shown.

The completed fly.

GROUSE/PARTRIDGE

There are a number of gamebirds in the world which fall into the grouse/partridge category, several of which are indigenous to North America. In the Northeast, we have the ruffed grouse, which many people call a partridge. In Maine and New Hampshire, that comes out "pahtridge." This bird has soft, nicely marked feathers which are well suited for making wet-fly hackles.

Actually, many gamebirds and some domestics have such plumage. Hen pheasants have soft, mottled feathers of varied shading, as do woodcock and various marsh birds. The markings vary, but as long as the size and texture are similar, any of these may be substituted for grouse or partridge.

Sale of the plumage of wild gamebirds is almost totally prohibited by law. Therefore, we must obtain these feathers from private sources, such as game preserves and friends who bird-hunt. English partridge feathers can be purchased from fly-tying supply houses. They tend toward a pale grey shade, which is okay for some patterns. But I like a more brownish cast. This can be obtained by dying the grey partridge hackles tan or light brown.

A few months ago (fall of 1984), a friend gave me the skin of some sort of European gamebird. Neither of us are sure just what it is—we think it's a Hungarian partridge—but oh, what feathers! They run to various shades of brown, are beautifully barred, and are the perfect size for the wet flies we tie. I will get hundreds of flies from that skin.

Saddles from domestic hens are also commercially available, and certain ones make very good grouse substitutes. The only problem I have with them is that the barbules tend to be extremely dense and webby—I guess that's too much of a good thing. When using such feathers, I strip off the barbules from one side of the center quill to avoid over-hackling the fly. This technique can be employed with any of these soft-hackle feathers when a more sparsely dressed fly is wanted.

ABOUT SYNTHETIC DUBBING

You will discover that some synthetics, such as the popular Andra Spectrum, are composed of extremely fine strands. While soft, this material has considerable tensile strength, which makes it difficult to pull excess dubbing from the thread. For this reason, it is advisable to make an extra effort not to spin on too much material.

Another problem this type of dubbing presents is that of patching or supplementation. Sometimes we want to add a tiny wisp to optimize a body, but when we attempt to select just the right amount, we come away with a long strand, more than we wanted.

Here are three ways to cope with this:
• Pull the strands apart, so they break in the middle.
• If that doesn't work, cut them.
• Fold or bunch the fibres and dub them onto the thread doubled or bunched.

As mentioned, it is sometimes necessary to supplement or add to a skein of dubbing in order to finish a body. The proper method is to spin on the additional material before wrapping all of the initial batch onto the hook. In other words, have some of the initial dubbing exposed so that when the supplement is added, it works in smoothly and evenly.

9

THE FUR-BODIED
SOFT-HACKLE

TECHNIQUES TO BE LEARNED

1. Spinning-loop dubbed body
2. Alternative methods for applying grouse hackle
3. Tinsel ribbing (option)

This is another marvelously effective variation on the soft-hackle theme. Practically any fur/feather combination can be utilized to obtain a variety of textures and shades. As an option, a flat or oval tinsel rib may be added to endow the fly with a bit of flash. I fish them both plain and ribbed.

For this and all dubbed-bodied flies, you will want to have the body material ready to go before you begin tying. The fur blend called for in this pattern can be purchased pre-mixed, or it can easily be prepared by the tyer. Instructions for doing this follow the tying steps.

As to hackles, the employment of techniques other than the conventional winding method we have studied up to now is extremely important. You have probably already noticed that finding the desired size of hackle requires a bit of sorting and scrutinizing. The smaller the fly, the more critical this becomes—and also the more frustrating because many types of feathers simply do not come in small sizes. This is particularly true of those used on soft-hackle flies and other types of wet flies and nymphs.

Examine a typical grouse, partridge, or similar gamebird skin and you will see that most of the feathers are too large for even the fairly sizeable flies we've been tying. What, then? Do we discard these otherwise lovely feathers? Hardly! We simply learn ways to make them work.

PATTERN DESCRIPTION

HOOK: Standard wet fly, size 10
THREAD: Black or brown pre-waxed

BODY: Fur from the face and ears of a hare or rabbit
HACKLE: Brown/grey mottled grouse or partridge feather

TYING STEPS

1. Mount the hook and tie on at approximately the midpoint of the hook shank. Wind the thread back nearly to the bend, perhaps one turn short of it.

2. Pull the bobbin downward so that approximately three inches (75 mm) of thread is exposed. Apply a thin coating of tacky wax such as Overton's Wonder Wax.

3. Start spinning small, fluffy bits of the fur blend onto the thread, beginning at the top. You want the fur to conform into a continuous, slightly tapered skein on the thread. Therefore, spin the fur loosely at first and do not pack the thread too tightly.

4. For this size hook, a two-inch (50 mm) length of fur is about right. It should be approximately the diameter of a piece of thin yarn, like Bernat mending yarn. The predominant mistake beginners make on dubbed bodies is to put on too much material.

5. Before proceeding to the next step, observe the fur on the thread. Are there any gaps? If so, fill them in by patching—that is, by spinning on the tiniest bunches of fur. Also, check to see that the upper end of the fur is almost in contact with the hook shank. If there is a gap, you can either slide the entire skein upward, or you can add a small amount of fur.

6. Now, with your left hand, grip the thread approximately ¼ inch (6 mm) below the lower end of the dubbed fur using hackle pliers, as shown.

7. While maintaining tautness by applying moderate tension with the pliers, pull out sufficient thread to reach up and over the hook shank.

8. Form the spinning loop by wrapping the thread around the hook, starting precisely where the downward thread is positioned, and winding forward.

Apply fur to thread gradually, in small quantities. Avoid using more material than is necessary.	Double the thread back up over the fur.	Wrap thread around hook at this position, thus completing loop.

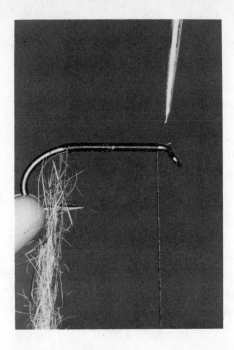

Advance thread to position indicated.

9. Wind forward to the position shown in the illustration. Note that we have allowed slightly less neck space than with the Basic Black. This is because we will be using a different hackle technique.

10. Let the bobbin hang and turn your attention to the hackle pliers. Let them hang, also. Hold the bobbin out of the way and twist the fur and thread loop by spinning the pliers in a clockwise direction. Usually, a couple of vigorous spins is sufficient—this will put several dozen twists into the spinning loop. You will know you have twisted enough when the loop resists further twisting and/or shows signs of bunching up next to the hook shank. If that actually happens, correct by un-twisting a turn or two.

11. Now begin to wrap the fur and spinning loop around the hook to form the body. Start at the very beginning of the bend—we left a tiny bit of space there, remember—and form a neat, well-packed body. You will probably need to tighten up a little after making a few wraps by applying several additional clockwise twists to the spinning loop.

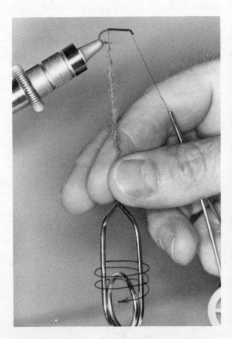 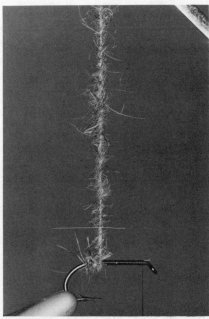

Spin hackle pliers clockwise. Note that bobbin and tying thread are held forward, out of the way.

Wrapping spun fur around hook. After completing the body, bind down and trim off the end of the spinning loop.

12. If all is in order, you will run out of fur just as you get to where the thread is hanging. Tie off the spinning loop as you have done with the body materials in the two previous patterns.

NOTE: If you have used too much fur and aren't able to tie off just the doubled thread of the spinning loop, here's what to do:

    A. Make one or two very firm wraps of tying thread around the spinning loop.

    B. Don't relax tension on the bobbin. Hold it above or on the far side of the fly, firmly.

    C. Let go of the hackle pliers, and let the remainder of the spinning loop untwist.

    D. Cut off the excess fur and thread. Try to clear out the throat area to leave space for hackle.

    E. Secure with several tight wraps.

13. Select a larger grouse feather, one with barbules which would be much too long if the hackle were wrapped in the fashion of the two previous flies.

14. Dispose of the fluffy waste material near the butt. Then stroke the fibres so that they stand out at a ninety-degree attitude from the center quill with the tips even.

15. Pull or cut off a bunch of barbules, about the same quantity as would be obtained with two turns of wrapped hackle.

Large grouse/partridge feather for hackle.

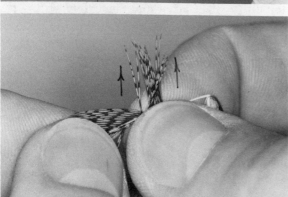

Preen and fold barbules to right angle from quill.

NOTE: Some feathers have less barbule density than others, and it is necessary to take fibres from both sides of the stem in order to obtain a sufficient amount. Simply use your hackle pliers as a handle. Grip the butt end of the stem with the pliers, grip the tip end with the left thumb and forefinger, and stroke all of the fibres into a bunch with the tips even. Then seize them with the left thumb and forefinger and cut or pull them from the stem. If you opt to pull off the fibres, trim the butts, as they tend to stick together, preventing the barbules from distributing themselves readily around the hook.

16. With the left thumb and forefinger, position the bunch of barbules on the far side of the neck, with the tips extending back to the rear of the body—or slightly short of it.

17. Now we will use the distribution wrap technique to cause the barbules to be deployed evenly around the entire circumference of the hook. Under virtually no tension, begin to wrap the thread slowly against and over the barbules. The idea is to tie down a few of them as you go, while the rest are driven ahead by the progression of the turn of thread. Help the process with the left hand by holding the fibres loosely and by encouraging them to be carried by the thread.

18. Apply a second wrap of thread under somewhat greater tension and examine the result. If there are gaps and bunches, roll the barbules around with the left thumb and forefinger so they

Position the barbules here, preparatory to beginning distribution wrap.

Barbules are distributed by thread movement, with assistance of fingers.

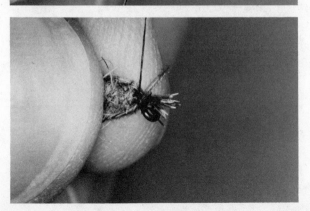

Start repeat wrap.

deploy more evenly. You can even unwind that second wrap of thread to abet this process, if necessary.

19. Survey the result once more. Are there any bald spots? You can patch with a few added barbules where needed.

20. Secure with several tight wraps, forming a neat head. During this process, try to force the hackles back against the front of the body, so as to induce them to flare and resemble a wrapped hackle. Don't create a long, unsightly neck, however.

21. Trim off the stub ends of the barbules as neatly as you can without nicking the thread. Now is when you will truly discover how good your scissors are.

22. Execute the whip-finish, apply head cement.

Increased thread tension induces barbules to distribute fully and evenly. Pressure against front of body causes hackle to flare.

The completed fly.

There is yet another method for hackling a fly with a bunch of fibres and the *slack loop* technique. It's a bit trickier than the one we just learned, but it produces a lovely effect when properly executed. Here are the tying steps:

1. Tie on near the eye, as before.

2. Select a feather and obtain a bunch of barbules.

3. With the left hand, hold the bunch against the hook with the *tips pointing forward*. Measure for proper length: the length of the shank plus a tiny bit more to allow for a few turns of thread.

Gauge for length.

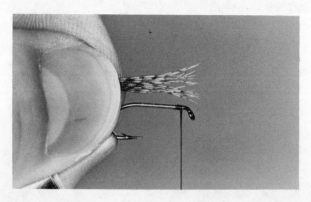

4. Hold the bunch of fibres at the neck of the hook, so that the measured hackle length extends beyond the front of the shank.

5. Execute the slack loop, then work the thread forward until it is only one or two turns behind the eye.

6. Wrap the thread to the rear and make a dubbed body, exactly as was done in the previous exercise. Be sure it reaches nearly to the eye.

7. With the left thumb and forefinger, pull back the bunch of fibres, keeping them evenly deployed around the hook. Then take a few wraps of thread in front of the fibres, forcing them back against the front of the body, until a wrapped-hackle effect is obtained.

8. Whip-finish, cement.

The two hackling methods you have just learned are of tremendous importance. Unless you become a dry-fly purist, you will be using one or both of these methodologies, and variations of them, to tie hackles on a wide variety of wet flies, nymphs, streamers, and even salmon flies. Just think of it—you can now create a hackle of appropriate size and conformation from almost any feather you pick up!

Let's examine the two flies you have just tied. Notice that the bodies are fairly smooth. I'm not about to say they won't take fish as they are—some smooth-body flies work very well. However, I prefer a little translucency. If you feel the same, fuzz up the bodies with your scroll saw blade. Go easy—we don't want to cut the thread that holds everything together.

Follow same distribution wrap procedure as before, but with barbules pointing forward.

Stroke back the hackle and make wraps of thread in front, working rearward.

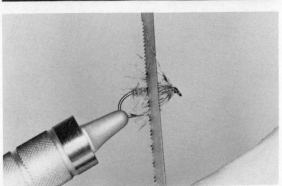

Fuzzing up the body with saw blade.

At this juncture, let's clarify a point. We have now learned the spinning-loop dubbing method, using fur, and the single-thread method, using synthetic material. This does not mean the criteria for choosing spinning-loop or single thread is whether one is dubbing fur or synthetics. The choice should be based on the characteristics of the material. That is why I left open the option of using synthetic or fur in the pattern description.

OPTION: TINSEL RIBBING

Here is the procedure for creating a tinsel rib.

1. After tying on and winding the thread to the rear of the hook, select a piece of flat mylar tinsel about four inches (100 mm) in length. It should be narrow. I recommend the 16/18 width, or the 14, if more flash is wanted.

2. Tie in the tinsel by holding it on top of the hook two or three thread-wraps from the bend. Use your left thumb to hold it flat. Pass the thread over the tinsel with moderate tension—then tighten—and secure with two more wraps, working toward the bend. This positions the tinsel on the far side of the hook and brings the thread to the point where the body will begin.

NOTE: Always have the side of the tinsel that you want to show facing outward. For this fly, I recommend the gold.

3. Construct the body, then make a series of evenly spaced wraps with the tinsel to form the ribbing. Five turns is considered traditional, but if four or six works out better, don't worry about it.

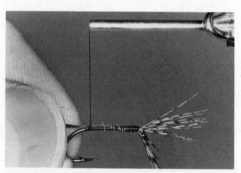

Tying in tinsel for ribbing.

Construct the body, stopping it just behind the grouse feathers.

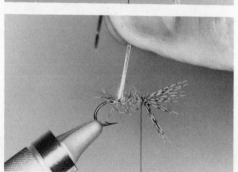

Keep tinsel rib well-spaced.

4. Tie off the tinsel beneath the throat with some good, tight wraps. Trim off the excess, and proceed with the hackle.

Tie tinsel off firmly, and keep the eye clear.

The completed fly.

PREPARATION OF HARE'S EAR DUBBING

The fur blend called for in this pattern is the same as that used on the ancient and famous Hare's Ear wet fly, which was transplanted here from Great Britain many years ago. While the name *Hare's Ear* has a poetic ring, the dubbing is taken primarily from the mask, as well as the ears and possibly certain parts of the body, although no purist would agree to the latter.

The idea is to obtain a rough, mottled, "tweedy" dubbing, with lots of guard hairs and only enough softer fur mixed in to make the material manageable. The spinning loop is the ideal technique for dubbing this coarse fur, as it locks the fibres firmly in place. Single-thread dubbing is great for soft, smooth materials, as we shall see, but it's a battle to get hare's ear dubbing onto a hook using the single-thread method, and it may not stay there very long when the fly is put into use.

As stated, dubbing should be prepared in advance. Lots of attractive fur blends are available commercially, but it's easy to do your own. There are two popular and effective methods: blending with a machine and felting in water.

BLENDING

This method requires a fur blender, which is nothing more than a small coffee mill or nut chopper. Fly-tying supply houses sell them at moderate cost. Regular kitchen blenders are poorly suited to this task because of the shape and location of the blades and the size of the receptacle.

To blend fur, simply cut, pull, or scrape it from the pelt, and zap it in the blender for a few seconds. It comes out fluffy and thoroughly mixed.

The method used for removing the fur from the pelt depends upon several factors. One of the most important ones is coloration. If you examine a rabbit skin, you will see that the color at the base is much different than that at the tips. Generally, it runs to a bluish grey. If a generous shading of grey is wanted, cut off the fur at the base. If not, cut it off somewhere in the middle. This method of controlling fur-blend coloration is applicable to nearly any type of pelt.

The hare's mask consists of fur and short, coarse guard hairs. This may be cut off or scraped off with a stiff, sharp razor blade. The ears have short, stiff hair, or *poll*. Scraping works best here.

Domestic bunny rabbits, such as the Eastern cottontail, don't have the beautiful masks of their overseas relatives, but there is still a great deal of usable dubbing on these animals. A very good blend may be obtained by discreetly selecting fur and guard hairs from different parts of the face and body and mixing them. And here is a neat trick for obtaining more coarseness and mottling, if desired: cut some hair from the backbone area of a squirrel pelt, and blend it in. Common grey squirrels are okay. Fox squirrels from the Midwest are super.

FELTING

If you don't have a fur blender, do not despair—you can get good results with nothing more than a bowl, a sieve, some warm water, and some liquid dishwashing detergent.

Take the fur and hair from the pelt, as described in the blender instructions. Place it in a jar, add luke-warm water and a few drops of detergent. Stir it around with a pencil or something similar. When the dubbing is all separated and floating free, pour it through a fine-mesh sieve. Then rinse with hot water until all traces of the detergent are removed. Note: If your sieve doesn't have a very fine mesh, put a coffee filter or paper towel in the bottom of it.

In the sieve you now have a round mass of felted fur. Dump it onto something absorbent, such as a thick layer of newspapers, overlaid with a couple of layers of paper towels to keep the newsprint from affecting the color of the fur. Put some more absorbent material over the fur and squeeze out the water with a rolling pin. Lay out the felted fur in a warm, dry place, and it will be ready to use quite soon.

Both the felting and blending methods can be used to create a wide variety of fur blends, including mixtures of fur and synthetic dubbing. However, discretion must be used when using the fur blender with synthetics. Some of them have very long fibres with great tensile strength and will bind the blades of the blender almost immediately. It doesn't take much to burn out a small electric motor.

10

THE BROWN HACKLE

TECHNIQUES TO BE LEARNED

1. Peacock herl body
2. Folding hackle

This is the fourth and last in our series of soft-hackle fly pattern lessons. It will teach two methods for constructing the popular peacock herl body, and also how to fold a hackle.

PATTERN DESCRIPTION

HOOK: Standard wet fly, size 10
THREAD: Black or brown, pre-waxed
BODY: Peacock herl
HACKLE: Soft rooster or hen, dark brown

TYING STEPS

1. Pull about six inches (150 mm) of extra thread out of the bobbin and tie on with that amount of excess. Wind to the bend. Secure the loose end of thread in the materials clip, or lacking that, drape it over the back of the vise.

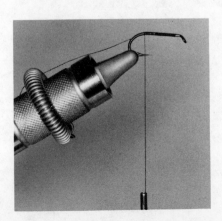

Note position of supplementary thread.

2. Select four or five fronds from a peacock tail. Use the ones on the stem, not those that form the multi-shaded eye portion.

3. Trim off the first half-inch (13 mm) or so of the tips. Then tie the feathers in by the tips at precisely where the excess thread meets the hook. Wrap the tying thread forward to a position about 1/16 of an inch (2 mm) behind the eye.

4. Retrieve the excess tag of thread and meld it in with the peacock fronds. Then take the thread and peacock together, and make only three or four clockwise twists at this point.

5. Make a wrap of the peacock/thread mixture around the hook. Now you may twist some more.

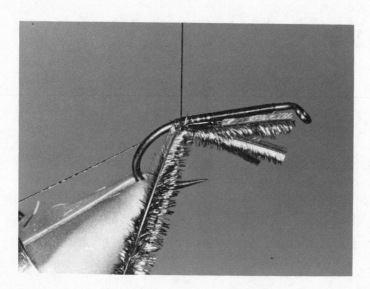

Tie in peacock, advance thread to position as shown.

Begin to twist peacock and supplementary thread together.

The first wrap.

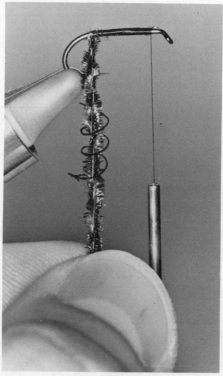
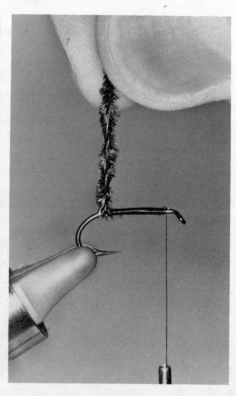

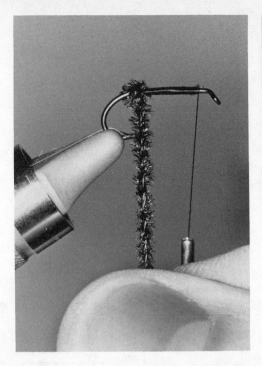

Tie off peacock well clear of eye.

Twist some more.

6. Continue to wrap forward, twisting as you go. Notice that the peacock/thread mixture takes on the appearance of chenille.

7. When the body is completed, tie off at the throat. Trim off and bind down the butt ends neatly, thereby creating a smooth foundation for the hackle.

8. Select a hackle feather of appropriate proportions for the hook size. Strip off the waste material, but leave the stem long so it can be used as a handle during the folding process.

9. Hold the butt end of the stem with the fourth and fifth fingers of the right hand. Use hackle pliers, if needed.

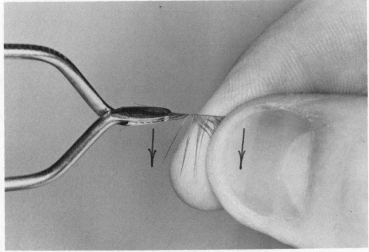

Barbules are stroked to one side of stem.

Hackle feather from hen cape ready to be folded.

10. Hold the tip of the feather with the left thumb and forefinger. Position the feather so that the bright side faces upward.

11. Using the right thumb and forefinger, stroke barbules downward and slightly rearward. Do not allow any barbules to cross over—make them stay on their side of the stem.

NOTE: Some feathers fold more readily if positioned with the dull side up. I was originally taught to do it this way, in fact. This is allowable on a fly of this type. On dressy flies, the maximum aesthetic effect is obtained by adhering to the bright-side-out method.

12. When the feather is folded, tie it in, stem underneath, with the barbules slanting rearward.

13. Begin to wrap the hackle as you did on the Basic Black. As you go, use the left hand to stroke the barbules back, thereby reinforcing the folded effect. Don't allow any barbules to fall ahead of the stem—force them all to slant rearward.

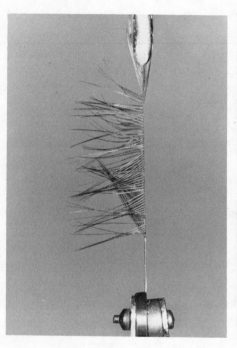

Folded hackle.

Tie in with all barbules pointing to the rear.

Stroke fibres back while winding hackle.

14. Take three to five turns of hackle, depending on how much you feel looks good.

15. Tie off, whip-finish, and cement.

The completed fly.

As I'm sure you've deduced, the reason for twisting the thread in with the feathers is to protect the stems, which are rather delicate. Here is another method. It requires fine copper wire, which may be obtained in a hobby shop or from someone who works on older electric motors.

1. Tie on and wrap to the bend. Then tie in a five-inch (125 mm) piece of the copper wire.

2. Tie in the peacock herl as before, and wrap to form a body.

3. Use the copper wire to create a *reverse* ribbing. In other words, wrap the wire toward yourself (counter-clockwise) so that the turns of wire cross over the turns of peacock.

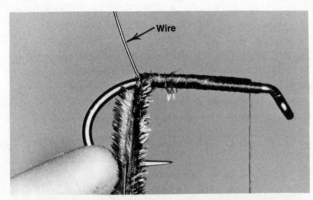

Alternative method for reinforcing peacock herl body. Note fine copper wire.

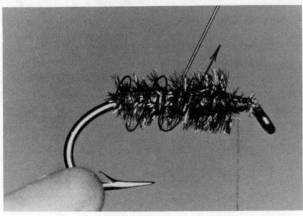

Wire is ribbed with reverse wraps— that is, counter-clockwise, looking at hook from the front.

4. Tie down and trim off the wire. Then proceed with the hackle.

When not using the twisted-thread method, the key to making a good-looking, fully packed body is to use enough fronds, at least four. Don't attempt to fill out the body by building up layers of herl—that doesn't work.

Newly shed peacock feathers are a deep iridescent green. Most of us feel this material looks fishier when it takes on a bronze caste. If green peacock is left by a window with exposure to the sun, it will eventually become bronze-ish.

Why fold hackle in the first place? It is not absolutely necessary—we did not do it on the Basic Black. Every year, many thousands of trout are caught on flies which don't have folded hackle. So why bother?

The answer—and I grant that it is somewhat subjective—is that folded-hackle flies look nicer. There seems to be general agreement on this. Aesthetics play a strong role in fly-tying, for we tie as much to please ourselves and our fellows as we do the fish. I know few tyers who do not strive to tie better-looking flies.

I also feel folded-hackle flies produce better, at least for me. Perhaps it's because I like their appearance and consequently fish them with a higher degree of optimism. Theodore Gordon is quoted, "Cast your fly with confidence." I believe this to be of tremendous importance in successful fly-fishing. I know that I fish better when I am genuinely charmed by the fly on the tip of my leader.

Here are some helpful hints on folding hackles:

- Try to select feathers with slender stems.
- Avoid using material down toward the butt of the feather for folded hackle. It folds poorly, and the thick stem will create a bulk problem.
- Be aware that some feathers fold well while others don't. So if you encounter a recalcitrant batch, don't blame yourself.
- Feathers that fold poorly may still be used to form a passable folded hackle by accentuating the stroking-back process during winding.
- Some feathers which can't be folded bright-side-out can be folded dull-side-out, and the appearance may suffer little, if at all.

11

THE WOOLY WORM

TECHNIQUES TO BE LEARNED

1. Chenille body, with optional wool butt and optional body weighting
2. Palmered-style hackle
3. Wooly Bugger variation

At first glance, the Wooly Worm might seem a retrogression. Not so. Several new disciplines come into play here, and without circumspection, not only might you have difficulty completing the fly—you might not be able to complete it at all!

Let me explain. Chenille is a bulky material and creates spacing problems for the tyer. Palmered hackle requires strict attention to the selection of an adequately long feather, as it must traverse the hook shank. Considering that the Wooly Worm is dressed on a longer-than-average hook, hackle selection is extremely critical, and the option of weighting the body exacerbates these difficulties.

This *is* the fifth pattern lesson, so let's go for broke and dress the fly with both options—though either or both may be omitted at the tyer's discretion. The Wooly Bugger pattern is a variation, rather than an option, and will be treated subsequently.

PATTERN DESCRIPTION

HOOK: 3X or 4X long, size 6, 8, or 10 (size 8 used in example)
THREAD: Black, pre-waxed
BUTT: Red yarn
BODY: Black chenille
WEIGHT: Fine lead wire
HACKLE: Black or grizzly, preferably saddle hackle

TYING STEPS

1. Tie on just in back of the eye. Wrap to the bend, then forward to a point approximately thirty percent of the shank length behind the eye.

2. Select a piece of red yarn about twice the length of the hook shank. Cut the front end on an angle and tie it in on top of the hook, as shown.

3. Pull the yarn taut with the left thumb and forefinger, then bind it to the hook shank, working the thread all the way to the bend.

4. Cut the yarn off, leaving a short butt.

5. Select a hackle and dispose of the waste at the butt. It must be rather long. For a size 6, 3X long hook, at least three inches (75 mm) of usable hackle is required, depending on the thickness of the chenille and whether or not the body is weighted.

6. Tie in the hackle at the bend. I suggest it be tied in by the tip, in order to effect a gradual taper, with the hackles becoming progressively longer as the feather is wound forward. However, some hackles are rather uniform in barbule length. So, examine your feather and decide whether or not you want to tie it in by the tip or butt.

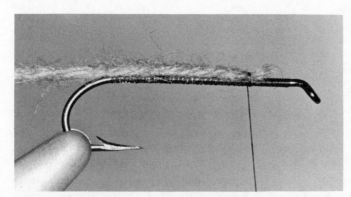

Tie on yarn here, wrap to bend,
cut off yarn to form tail.

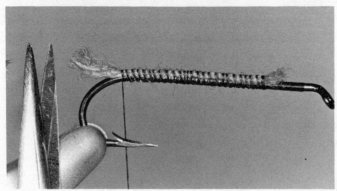

Chenille prepared for tying in.

Hackle tied in by tip.

Leave adequate
room at front—chenille
is bulky.

7. Select a piece of fine- or medium-thickness black chenille, approximately six inches (150 mm) in length. With your thumbnail, scrape off a little of the fuzz at one end, exposing perhaps a quarter inch (6 mm) of the thread core.

8. Tie in the chenille by the core—thus avoiding a lot of bulk at this point. Secure the hackle and chenille in the materials clip, then wrap the thread forward to ¹⁄₁₆ of an inch (less than 2 mm) behind the eye.

9. Select a piece of fairly fine lead wire, seven or eight inches (175–200 mm) in length.

NOTE: At no point is the thread involved in fastening the lead wire. Hold the wire behind the hook shank approximately twenty percent forward from the bend and wrap it around the shank, using neat, contiguous wraps.

10. Wrap the wire forward to a point one or two turns beyond where the yarn was tied in and simply break or cut it off. Do likewise with the tag end at the rear. *Soak* with head cement.

Position lead wire behind hook,
wrap forward.

Apply cement generously.

Wrapping the body.

Chenille is one of the most difficult materials to trim and tie off without blocking the eye. Try to work on far side of hook. Leave space for tying off hackle.

11. Retrieve the chenille and wrap it forward, leaving sufficient space to tie it off without crowding the eye.

12. Wrap the hackle over the chenille, using evenly spaced turns, as shown. You will get six to eight turns depending on how widely they are spaced.

13. Tie off, whip-finish, cement.

The completed fly.

Palmer-style hackle being wound. Note spacing.

Now the Wooly Bugger variation:

1. For an unweighted fly, simply tie on near the front and wrap to the bend. For a weighted version, follow the procedure for the Wooly Worm, remembering to first tie on the marabou tail and then tie in the chenille and hackle.

2. Select a black marabou feather and cut off a bunch sufficient to make a nice, full tail. Remember that marabou slims down a great deal when wet, so don't be too skimpy.

3. Tie on the marabou at the bend using the pinch. Tail length is up to the tyer. One to one-and-a-half times the body length, give or take a little, seems to work nicely.

Marabou (turkey) feathers of two types.

Obtaining material from large feather.

Obtaining material from short feather.

Bunch of marabou for tail, in position for tie-on.

NOTE: If you have weighted the body, cut off the marabou butts at the point where the wire starts. On an unweighted body, tie them down along the top of the hook, so a big bump isn't formed near the bend. This is slightly cumbersome. The suggested method is to hold them taut with the right hand, just the reverse of the wool butt process, then use the left hand to make the thread wraps, passing the bobbin over the top, releasing it, and catching it coming underneath. Trim at about twenty percent behind the eye, then wrap back to the bend. (Marabou is less cumbersome, too, if you wet it slightly.)

4. Tie in the chenille and hackle, and finish the fly as per instructions for the Wooly Worm.

The Wooly Bugger.

ABOUT MARABOU

When purchasing marabou, you may encounter two distinctly shaped types of feathers. One has a pronounced stem running virtually the full length. The other is shorter and consists mostly of plumage, with a much less conspicuous stem. These are called *shorts* or *bloods,* and I prefer them for most applications. The entire end section may be utilized, as the center quill is not so thick as to affect the appearance or action of the plumage.

In this pattern lesson we have seen that with a simple variation we can sometimes convert a fly into one having distinctly different properties. The Wooly Worm is generally suggestive of subaquatic insect life, while the Wooly Bugger simulates leeches, elvers, and perhaps certain baitfishes. It is also an impressionistic attractor, particularly when dressed in bright colors. Both of these patterns are great fish-takers.

12

THE MUSKRAT NYMPH

TECHNIQUES TO BE LEARNED

- Nymph-type tail
- Nymph body shaping
- Thorax
- Wing case
- Legs/hackle—two methods

The Muskrat is a time-proven general nymph pattern. It can be dressed in a range of sizes, weighted or not, and with or without tinsel ribbing. If these options are employed, use the finest lead wire and tinsel. On small nymphs, gold or silver wire may be used for ribbing. The example will be dressed plain and unweighted. However, I will indicate at which point the various steps for weighting and ribbing should be executed.

We are working on a 2X-shank hook with this pattern, and the proportions will be considerably different than with the soft-hackle series of flies. For this reason, the quantities and dimensions of the components are explicit.

PATTERN DESCRIPTION

HOOK: Size 10 or 12, 2X long
THREAD: Black, pre-waxed
TAIL: Grey hen or soft rooster barbules
BODY: Grey muskrat fur or substitute
THORAX: Same
WING CASE: Selection of dark grey duck or goose wing feather
LEGS/HACKLE: Dark grey hen or soft rooster barbules

TYING STEPS

1. Tie on a little ways back from the eye and wind to the bend. If a weighted body is desired, apply the lead wire at this point, as was done on the Wooly Worm.

2. For the tail, select a small bunch of grey hackle fibres, either hen or webby rooster. Stroke them out straight from the stem so that the tips are even, and cut or pull them from the stem.

3. The tail on this nymph should be a webby wisp, about half the shank length. Tie it in at the very bend, using the pinch. Try to get the fibres to spread. It is helpful to create a small bump, using a few wraps of thread, right at the bend. The tail is tied in just ahead of this, so that the bump causes the fibres to flair.

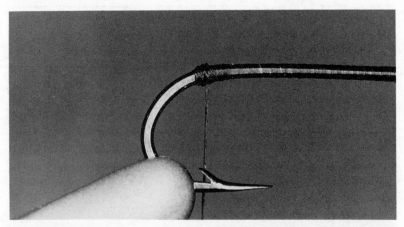

Thread bump to aid in spreading tail fibres.

Tail tied on, fibres spread.

4. If tinsel ribbing is desired, tie it in now.

5. The body may be constructed using either the spinning-loop or single-thread dubbing technique. Personally, I prefer the spinning loop for this type of fly. In either case, spin about 2½ inches (63 mm) of fur onto the thread to form a distinct taper. If the spinning loop is opted for, use more dubbing, as it will pack tighter. If the single-thread method is used, wrap the thread forward and then back to bind down the excess tail material. This is not necessary with the spinning loop since the material is bound down as a matter of course when the tying thread is wrapped forward.

6. Wind the thread forward to a point thirty-five to forty percent back from the eye.

7. Construct the dubbed body, stopping when the tying thread is reached. If ribbing with tinsel, do so at this point. Only the body itself is ribbed—the thorax, which will be constructed subsequently, is not ribbed.

8. The wing case is made out of a strip from a dark-grey goose or duck wing quill. It needs to be treated with some adhesive, for durability. A thin smear of Pliobond is very good, as it never gets completely hard. Or, the entire feather may be sprayed with an artist's material called Tuffilm, then separated into wing cases, as needed. If you choose not to apply adhesive to the feather, coat it with four layers of head cement after the fly is completed.

9. The strip should be about 5/32 inches (4 mm) wide. Tie it in directly on top of the hook, holding it flat with the thumb. Be sure it is centered. Trim the excess and bind down the stub.

NOTE: You will be folding the strip over the thorax, so the side you want to show must be facing *down*.

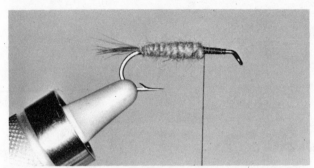

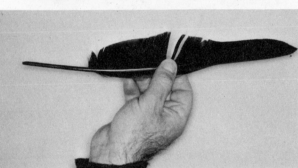

Dubbed body. Note proportions.

Selecting a wing-case strip from goose or duck feather.

Wing-case strip being tied in. Maintain full width of feather strip, and keep it flat atop hook.

10. Apply more dubbing and make a thorax. It should be contiguous to the front of the body and slightly thicker. Wrap the dubbing very snugly against the feather strip, and make it thickest at this point to help form a sightly wing case. Leave about ⅟₁₆ inch for the legs between the thorax and the eye.

11. The legs consist of a bunch of webby, dark-grey hen or rooster barbules. They will be deployed around the sides and throat using the distribution wrap technique. Hold the bunch against the far side of the hook with the left forefinger, then wrap the thread, allowing the fibres to travel with it. Some will be tied down, the rest will continue on around the hook to the throat and the near side. Help them along with the left forefinger, if required.

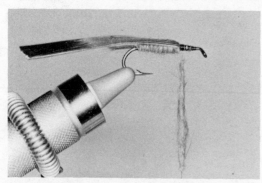

Wing-case strip tied in, dubbing for thorax in place.

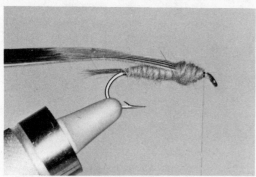

Completed thorax.

Proportions for legs/hackle.

Legs in place via distribution wrap.

12. When the barbules are distributed as shown, tie them down with four or five tight wraps and trim off the butts.

13. Now fold the feather strip over the thorax to form the wing case. It is helpful to fold it over a needle, in order to obtain a nice squared-off effect at the rear.

14. Tie down the wing case—be careful not to allow the feather to fold over itself. Trim, whip-finish, cement. For greater durability, you may wish to apply several coatings of head cement to the wing case, also.

Folding the wing case forward.

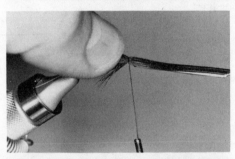

Use thumb to hold wing case flat while tying it down.

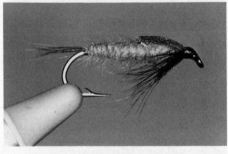

Completed fly, side view and top view.

Applying head cement to wing case.

OPTION: ALTERNATIVE METHOD FOR APPLYING LEGS

Some tyers seek to obtain a bit more realism by using a small feather, folded over the thorax with the barbules protruding on either side. Here's the process:

1. After tying in the wing-case feather and before making the thorax, select a small dark-grey hackle, preferably hen. Prepare it by disposing of the waste near the butt and by stroking the fibres outward to ninety degrees from the stem, as we did with the grouse feather in the Olive/Grouse Soft-Hackle. The amount of hackle is determined by the distance from the front of the body to just behind the eye—in other words, that's how long the barbule-covered stem should be.

2. Tie in the feather with the dull, or concave side, facing up and the butt pointing rearward. It should be secured tightly against the wing-case feather and the front of the body.

3. Make the thorax as described. Then seize the stem and fold the hackle feather over the thorax, taking care to center the stem.

Soft feather for fold-over hackle, flared and trimmed for tying in. Note how length of portion to be used for legs is determined.

Legs/hackle feather in place. Note that it abuts the body.

Legs/hackle feather folded forward over thorax and tied down.

Top view of completed fly.

4. Tie down the stem and trim it off. Then fold the wing case over and complete the fly, per instructions.

There are many other methods for dressing nymphs, but quite frankly, if you want to keep things simple, the processes just described are about all you will ever need to know. Variations of this simple nymph are practically infinite, in terms of size, color, hook length and shape, leg and hackle material, and silhouette. Practically any nymphal form can be effectively represented in this manner.

13

THE MARCH BROWN WET FLY

TECHNIQUES TO BE LEARNED

1. Flank-feather fibre wing and emerger option
2. Optional quill-section wing
3. Thread ribbing
4. Beard-style hackle

The March Brown dates back almost to the very infancy of British fly-tying, as it was created to simulate an important mayfly native to the streams of the British Isles. The American March Brown is a different insect, although not entirely dissimilar. Where habitat degradation has not been too pervasive, it is still a fly of major interest to the angler and is one certainly worth having in the fly box.

As with most patterns, there are various ways to tie the March Brown. In this exercise, we will learn two common techniques for tying the wet-fly wing. Once mastered, these methods will open up a host of patterns to the tyer.

Up to now, we have dressed generally suggestive types of flies. Here, we are trying to imitate a particular insect. The dressing I prescribe is one that works where I do *my* fishing. However, it should be kept in mind that stream insects vary remarkably from habitat to habitat. Thus, your March Browns may be larger, smaller, darker, or lighter than mine. Learn to be observant and tie what you see—or what you think the fish sees.

PATTERN DESCRIPTION

HOOK: Size 8 or 10, 1X long
THREAD: Brown or white, pre-waxed
TAIL: Grouse fibers
RIBBING: Dark brown thread, heavy
BODY: Cream or light tan dubbing, fur or synthetic
WINGS: Brown mallard flank feather fibers
HACKLE: Grouse fibres

TYING STEPS

1. Tie on about twenty-five percent of the shank length behind the eye, and wrap to the bend. Then tie in a webby wisp of grouse barbules, or something similar, for the tail. It should be about half the shank length and not too bulky.

2. Tie in a four-inch (100 mm) piece of brown thread for the ribbing.

3. Make a cigar-shaped dubbed body, using either spinning loop or single thread. Your choice of method might depend on the properties of the dubbing material you have selected. Build a nice front taper into the body, so that it will not interfere with tying in the wings later on. Leave yourself 1/16 inch (2 mm) for the hackle and wings—or even a hair more.

4. Wind the ribbing and tie it off.

5. Select a grouse feather with long barbules, as in the Fur-Bodied Soft-Hackle, and stroke the fibers to a right angle from the center quill. Cut or pull off a bunch, keeping the tips fairly even.

6. Position the bunch at the throat, just behind the eye. Adjust the length—a good rule of thumb is that they should cover the hook point and extend almost to the barb.

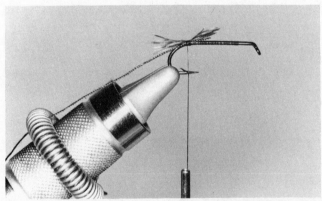

Tail and ribbing thread in place.

Ribbing being applied.

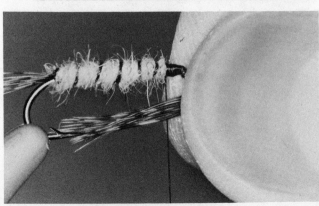

Position bunch of barbules at throat. Note length.

7. Tie in the bunch with an inverted pinch—that is, the thread is brought up from directly below, between the pinched thumb and forefinger. Secure with several tight wraps—be careful not to work up against the eye. Trim off the excess.

8. For the wing, select a brown mallard feather of mixed brown-and-grey coloration. Stroke a generous bunch of fibers at an angle from the stem so that the tips are fairly even. Cut them off close to the stem.

Tie in the bunch with an upside-down pinch.

The completed hackle.

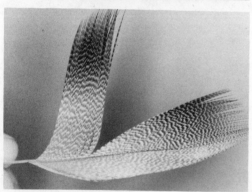

Preparing brown mallard feather for use as wing material.

Section of brown mallard, removed from quill.

9. You are now holding a section of fibers with your left thumb and forefinger. The section is lying flat, with the cupped side down. Fold it in the middle by coming down with the right thumb and forefinger over the butts, meanwhile gradually relaxing your grip with the left hand. You will end up with a folded bunch held by the butt end between the right thumb and forefinger.

10. Position the folded bunch directly on top of the hook. Length should be even with the rear extremity of the hook. Do *not* let the wings extend to the end of the tail.

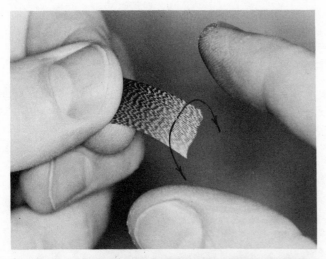

Folding mallard section. Hold by tip end with left hand, stroke downward with right thumb and forefinger.

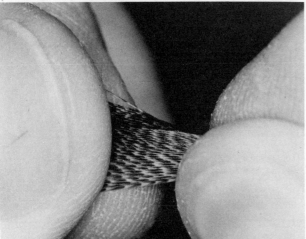

Position folded bunch atop hook. Note length.

11. Tie down the wings with a pinch, followed by a second pinch directly in front of the first one. Remove your left hand, and see how the wings look. If not satisfied, seize the bunch again, unwrap, and repeat the process. When the desired result is obtained, secure the wings with several tight wraps while stabilizing them with the left thumb and forefinger.

12. Trim off the excess and police the area with a few discreet wraps of thread. Whip-finish, cement.

NOTE: The head should be dark brown. If your thread is not of that shade, use a felt marker to touch it up.

Wing secured in place, excess being trimmed.

The completed fly.

EMERGER OPTION

Sometimes we want to simulate an emerging fly that is having difficulty extricating itself from the nymphal case or that has not yet received sufficient blood supply to the wings to cause them to fill out. A number of ingenious innovations have been developed that include tying on a short section of marabou or a small piece of nylon stocking. The easiest method is simply to tie the wing we just learned, half-length. The fibres are finer near the tips. If your emerger wings look too sparse, supplement them by tying another bunch on top of the first.

ABOUT FLANK FEATHERS

Brown mallard makes lovely wings, but if you don't have any, do not despair—teal and plain mallard flank feathers are excellent substitutes. They do not have the brownish cast called for in this fly pattern, so you may wish to touch them up a bit by stippling them with a waterproof dark-brown felt pen.

With teal and common mallard, you will find many feathers with symmetrical tip sections. These also make nice wet-fly wings. They are folded, just like the fibre sections taken from the sides. The center quill does not extend to the tip and is consequently not a factor.

Barred wood duck, that precious commodity, is prescribed for many great fly patterns. It is handled in the same manner as the feathers previously mentioned. For your fledgling efforts, I suggest practicing with dyed mallard. In fact, for wet flies, I find dyed mallard perfectly suitable.

WING-QUILL SECTION OPTION

For centuries, fly-tyers have fashioned wings using strips or sections of feathers from various birds, with beautiful results. Grey duck and goose quills are used on a multitude of patterns, due to the predominance of grey or slate as the wing coloration of common stream insects. However, the March Brown happens to have a mottled brown-grey wing, so we will obtain our sections from turkey quills of similar coloration.

Turkey wing quills vary from duck and goose wing quills, in that quite frequently the stem is more or less centered, so that opposing sections may be taken from either side of the quill. This is never so with duck or goose, where it is necessary to use two feathers—one from the left wing and one from the right—so that the two sections have opposing curvature and match up properly.

However, not all turkey quills are symmetrical enough to produce matched winging strips from one feather, in which case you will need two similar quills from opposing wings, as with goose and duck.

Here are the steps for constructing quill-section wings for our March Brown wet fly:

1. From a single symmetrical turkey quill or from two similar but opposing ones, cut out two narrow sections. They should be approximately ³⁄₁₆ of an inch wide near the quill. It is of great importance that the widths be *exactly equal*.

A centered-quill turkey feather.
Sections for two sets of wings
have been cut out.

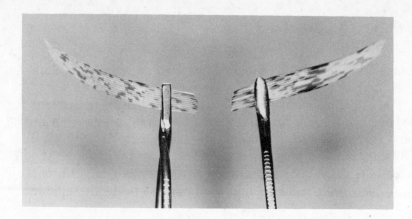

Wing sections with opposing curvature.

2. The sections are matched cupped side to cupped side. Hold them by the butts, one between the right thumb and forefinger, the other between the forefinger and middle finger, as shown.

3. Manipulate the feathers, causing the tips to come together. When they are matched up perfectly, grasp the tips with the left thumb and forefinger.

4. Align the two sections, so that the strips lie together as one for their full length.

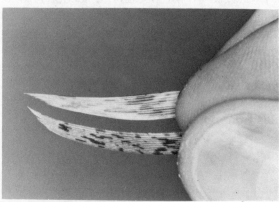

Hold sections with concave sides facing, using right thumb, forefinger and middle finger, as shown. Bring tips together with "chopsticks" movement. Seize by tip ends with left hand, then reseize by butt ends with right hand and position atop hook.

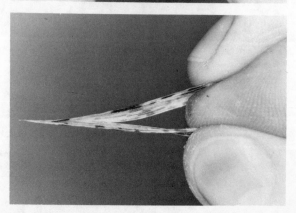

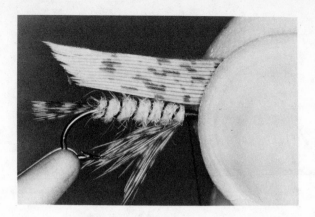

5. Take the strips in the right hand and set them precisely atop the hook, gauging the length in accordance with previous instructions.

6. Execute the pinch and re-pinch, and perhaps a third. Observe the effect and either secure with several tight wraps or unwind the thread, adjust the quills, and repeat the pinches.

NOTE: With either type of wing, it is important that the wraps used to secure the wings are taken in *front* of the first pinch.

7. Trim the quill sections. Hold the wings securely with the left hand to prevent them from rolling or twisting while making the final thread wraps. Finish off the fly.

If you can tie the seven flies we have studied—and the options—you have an excellent working knowledge of wet-fly design and construction. You would be shocked to learn how many patterns you can now dress by mixing and matching, but that's for a later chapter. Let us now direct our attention to another school of subsurface fly-tying: the streamer.

The completed fly.

14

THE GOLDEN DARTER

TECHNIQUES TO BE LEARNED

1. Basic streamer silhouette
2. Floss body with tinsel ribbing
3. Feather wing, with marabou option
4. Imitation Jungle Cock
5. Weighted body—alternative method

The streamer, though first tied in England, is uniquely American; it flourished because of the carnivorous tendencies of our native brook trout and the abundance of small forage fish in our trout streams and lakes. The Golden Darter was conceived by Lew Oatman, a superb fly-tyer and fly-designer who met an untimely death in 1958.

Some of the great streamer-fly designers have tended to be considerably more abstract in their designs than those in the dry-fly/nymph school. Many streamer patterns are semi or total attractors, dressed for unsophisticated trout in seldom-fished habitats. However, there is an imitative school of streamer design whose exponents pay as much attention to realism as do their insect-oriented counterparts. This group includes such luminaries as Carrie Stevens, Sam Slaymaker, Polly Rosborough, Keith Fulsher, Don Gapen, and the aforementioned Mr. Oatman.

While not a strict imitator, the Golden Darter was designed to represent baitfish that Lew observed in his beloved Battenkill. This is exemplified by his choice of badger hackle feathers for the wings, which feature a dark stripe down the center. Such markings are prominent on the black-nosed dace and certain other common minnows.

We shall be using a hook which is considerably longer and (hopefully) somewhat stronger than those in previous pattern lessons. If your vise does not hold this type of hook securely with the jaws gripping only the bottom portion of the bend, you may insert the barb and even the point, if necessary.

102

PATTERN DESCRIPTION

HOOK: Size 8, 6X long streamer
THREAD: Yellow or white, pre-waxed
TAIL: Turkey quill section
BODY: Yellow floss
RIBBING: Gold tinsel, fine or medium-fine
THROAT: Teal fibers
WINGS: Golden badger hackles
SHOULDERS: Jungle Cock imitation, per instructions
NOTE: Mr. Oatman's original dressing calls for a Jungle Cock body feather throat and Jungle Cock nails or eyes for the shoulders. Jungle Cock is not legally available in the United States, so we shall innovate.

TYING STEPS

1. Tie on twenty-five percent of the shank lenth behind the eye, and wrap to the bend. Use neat, contiguous wraps. I realize this is time-consuming, but with sensitive body materials, such as floss and tinsel, the extra effort pays dividends in a smooth, lovely-to-look-at body, with no "read-through" from ridges of thread underneath.

2. Tie on a tail consisting of a section of turkey quill, just like that used on the optional March Brown wing. It should be short, approximately the gape of the hook in length. Use the pinch technique. Don't chop off the excess, trim it on the bias—it will be bound down to form a nicely tapered underbody.

3. Select a fine or medium-fine piece of tinsel, five inches (125 mm) in length, and tie it in as you did on the Fur-Bodied Soft-Hackle, gold side out. Again, don't chop off the excess at the last wrap—cut it about where you originally tied on near the front.

Tail and ribbing tinsel tied in.
The technique for mounting the tail
is the same as that for the turkey
wings on the March Brown wet fly.

4. Bind down the excess tail feather material and tinsel to form the underbody. Be neat with the thread wraps, working forward to a position 3/32 of an inch (2.5 mm) behind the eye. Coat the underbody with a thin layer of head cement.

5. You are about to handle floss, a material which is easily soiled. Be sure your hands are clean and free of body oils, fly-tying wax, or other contaminant.

6. Select a ten-inch (250 mm) length of medium-thickness yellow floss. Tie it in at the thread position, against the bottom of the hook, using an inverted pinch. Secure with several tight wraps, trim off the excess.

7. Begin to wrap the floss rearward, with each wrap slightly overlapping the previous one. You will notice it has a tendency to flatten or spread, which is desirable. However, do not allow individual strands to become separated from the rest. If this happens, back off a turn or two and regroup the floss.

NOTE: It is often helpful to wiggle floss back and forth a bit as you wrap. This abets even distribution.

8. At the bend, start working the floss forward over the first layer. When the thread position is reached, tie off the floss beneath the hook with several tight wraps, then trim neatly.

Tie in floss at throat. Note space allowed for subsequent operations.

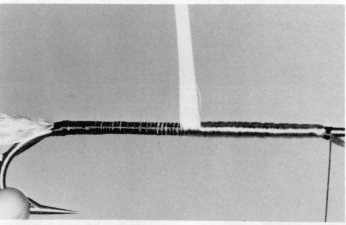

Start wrapping floss rearward.

Reverse at tail and wrap floss forward over first layer. Floss may spread somewhat, but do not allow individual strands to separate themselves from the skein.

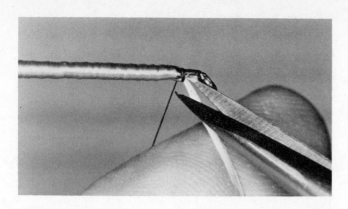

Floss is slippery. Be sure it is locked in before cutting off excess.

9. Retrieve the tinsel and wind the rib, using neat, evenly spaced spirals. Don't make them too close together—the floss should predominate. On a size 8, 6X hook, you will get eight or nine turns.

10. Tie off the tinsel at the throat with three or four tight wraps. Work the thread forward to lock in the tinsel.

11. Select a bunch of barred teal—or lacking that, barred mallard—and tie in a short beard-style hackle. See the illustration for the correct proportions.

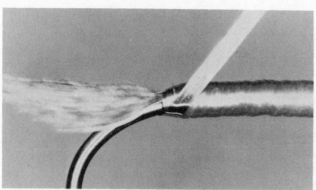

Starting the tinsel.

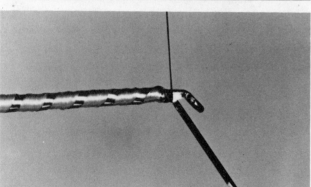

Tying off the tinsel. Again, lock it in well.

Throat hackle in place.

Wing feathers. Note opposing curvature.

12. Select two golden badger hackles, either cape or saddle. They must be long enough that when the waste is removed, the usable portion will be about 1½ times the shank length.

NOTE: The feathers should be as alike as possible in shape and marking. If the feathers are straight, any matched pair will do. If they are curved, select one from the right side of the cape or saddle and one from the left, so that, when faced dull-side to dull-side, the curvature matches.

13. Face the feathers dull-sides-in, and match up the tips. While holding them firmly, strip the excess from both feathers at once, so they are perfectly analogous. Trim the stems to about ½ inch (12 mm).

NOTE: Don't get carried away when stripping—you can't put the barbules back on the quill once they are gone.

14. Place the feathers atop the hook with the front of the feathered portion about ³⁄₃₂ inches (2.5 mm) back from the eye. Check for proper length, strip off more fibers if necessary.

NOTE: If working with curved feathers, mount them so that the curvature slopes downward toward the rear, as illustrated.

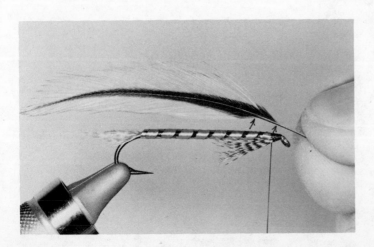

Wing feathers prepared for mounting.
Note that more barbules have been removed from the bottom of the stem than the top.

15. When satisfied with the wing length, strip off a few more barbules from the bottom of the stems, perhaps ⅛ inch (3 mm). This helps prevent the wing from cocking, or pointing upward at too great an angle.

16. Apply a drop of cement to the spot where the wings will be mounted. Then re-set the wings atop the hook in their final position. Do not allow the stems to cross over each other at the point where they will be tied down. If they cross in front of the hook, no problem.

17. Hold the feathers so that the stems lie side by side against each other, and center them on top of the hook. Locate your first wrap of thread at a position which will allow two more wraps rearward to the front of the feathered portion. Do not use the pinch—the stems are sufficiently stiff that they won't roll, unless too much thread tension is applied.

18. Make three thread wraps as follows: the first is merely snug, the second tighter, and the third tighter still. Hold the wings in position throughout the wrapping.

Wings mounted. When trimming off quills, hold wings firmly in place with left thumb and forefinger.

19. Let go of the wings, and see how they look. If satisfied, secure them with several firm wraps and trim off the stems just behind the eye. Hold the wings firmly to prevent them from rolling. This is particularly critical while cutting off the stems.

NOTE: Sometimes streamer wings have a tendency to roll to either side, so that a "V" is formed between the two wings. This may be caused by not having created an adequate thread base—in other words, you are trying to tie down the stems on too narrow a platform. If this occurs, remove the wings and build up the base with some discreet wraps of thread. Then add another small drop of head cement, and try again. This is one of the few situations where I will suggest being a bit generous with the tying thread.

20. For the shoulders, we will fashion imitation Jungle Cock eyes out of guinea-fowl feathers—an inexpensive and readily obtainable material. These feathers are black with white dots. Select two of them which have dots centered on the quill.

Guinea fowl feather for making imitation Jungle Cock eye. Note white dot centered on quill.

21. Strip off the fibres until the centered dot is isolated. Then trim to an elongated oval shape, as shown.

NOTE: There is a burner available designed expressly for this task. It works great. If you are going to be making a lot of these eyes, I suggest you obtain one.

22. Tie on the near-side eye first. Hold it flat against the wing, with the white dot centered on the black stripe. Use a gentle wrap of thread, followed by a firm one. Survey the result. If the eye has rolled, unwrap and re-tie—this time catching the very front of the fibres, as well as the stem. This is how real Jungle Cock eyes are tied on.

Feather mounted in burner.

Imitation Jungle Cock eyes after removal from burner.

Mounting eye on cheek of fly.

23. Tie on the far-side eye in similar fashion. Be sure it is the same length as the near one and is centered on the black stripe.

24. Trim the stems, make a neat, tightly wrapped head. Color it black with a waterproof felt marker, whip-finish, and cement.

Far-side eye is a mirror image of near-side eye.

The completed fly.

The same fly with real Jungle Cock feathers being tied on.

MARABOU-WING AND WEIGHTED-BODY OPTIONS

The marabou-wing option is my own, not Lew Oatman's. It produces a somewhat different look—there's no other coloration to the wing, just the black—but, it takes fish! Concurrently, let's learn another method for adding weight to a streamer body—one which works well with floss.

1. Tie on and wind to the bend, then wind forward to a point about twenty percent of the shank length behind the eye. Coat the wrappings with head cement.

2. Select a piece of thick lead wire, at least equal in diameter to the hook shank. It should be long enough to extend from the thread location to just short of the beginning of the bend. Taper the two ends.

3. Hold the wire against the bottom of the hook shank and wrap over it to the bend.

4. Tie on a black marabou tail one half the body length, as in the Wooly Bugger. Then tie in the tinsel ribbing and wrap forward to the throat, as previously instructed. Cover the wrappings with a thin coat of head cement.

5. Tie in the throat, as before.

6. Select a bunch of black marabou 1¼ to 1½ times the shank length. Avoid overly long marabou wings, they will wrap themselves around the hook during casting. The marabou tail acts as a wing supplement.

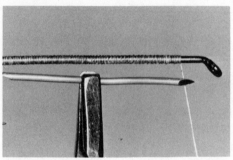

Lead strip prepared for tying on.

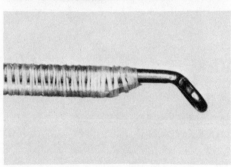

Lead strip in place.

Marabou tail in place. Note length.

Mounting the marabou wing.
After locking in the wing, trim all
excess, so that hook eye is not obscured.

NOTE: Marabou wings should be dressed fairly generously, as this material slims down remarkably when wet. It is not good practice to tie overly thick bunches of bulky material onto a hook—both strength and aesthetics are compromised. Consequently, I suggest tying on the marabou in two equal bunches on larger flies or where extra-full dressing is required.

7. Tie the required amount of marabou, using the pinch. Secure with several tight wraps, and trim.

8. Wrap the head, color it black, whip-finish, and cement.

The completed fly, dry.

The completed fly, wet.

ADDITIONAL NOTES

The body-weighting method demonstrated in this pattern lesson does not add as much weight as wrapped lead wire, but it is much easier to construct a floss or tinsel body over it. After some practice, you can add more weight by tying on another strip of wire after thread-wrapping the first one. I do not rule out using the wrapped-wire method—however, the wire must be very fine, and the floss must be of sufficient thickness to fill in the "step" where the wire begins.

Sometimes appearance and effectiveness are improved by using double feather wings, particularly on larger flies. This requires two matched pairs, which brings into play a few more stringent disciplines. All four feathers must match in size, shape, and markings. If there is curvature, the two feathers which form the near wing and the two which form the far wing must be similarly shaped. Since you now have four stems to deal with, there must be sufficient thread base on which to mount them. You might consider obtaining some looped-eye hooks, which have a much wider and flatter mounting surface.

While the Jungle Cock shoulder is considered optional in some quarters, my experience indicates that it definitely contributes to a streamer fly's effectiveness. Some tyers find it easier to pre-assemble the shoulders and wings—no less an authority than Carrie Stevens of Grey Ghost fame was an advocate of this procedure.

All that's entailed is gluing the shoulder feather to the wing feather ahead of time and allowing the assembly to dry. Of course, care must be taken to position the shoulders accurately since they cannot be adjusted later. The adhesive should be quick drying and not too runny—we do not want it to bleed into the wing feather beyond the immediate point of attachment. Pliobond, while slightly messy, is an excellent adhesive for such applications.

One last word on feathers for streamer wings. Some tie on perfectly with no special effort, as though nature designed them just for that purpose. Others twist, roll, and do everything except what the tyer would like. Sometimes these feathers can be coaxed, and after a few manipulations and re-tries, they will behave. A bit of discreet stem-flattening with pliers may help. Another trick is to try turning them over, provided curvature doesn't rule this out. But over time, you will find that some capes and saddles simply do not produce feathers which tie down well. If there is a way to accurately identify these negative tendencies by observation alone, I am not aware of it.

I mentioned that marabou wings, if dressed a bit too long, will wrap themselves around the hook during casting. This is true of other streamer wing materials, to a lesser degree. In the case of marabou, there are a couple of tricks one can use when a longer wing is desired:
- Tie in a sparse underwing of stiffer material, such as bucktail or synthetic hair, about the length of the body.
- Substitute a marabou tail as in the marabou-wing option. When wet, the wing and tail will appear to meld, looking almost like one long bunch.

It goes without saying that as larger hooks are used, more material is required—body material in particular. I specified lengths for floss and tinsel based on a size 8, 6X long hook. Add roughly ten percent for each step up in hook size.

15

THE MICKEY FINN

TECHNIQUES TO BE LEARNED

1. Tinsel body with oval ribbing
2. Hairwing and synthetic hair substitute
3. Optional tubular mylar body, weighted
4. Optic head, optional

Now we will dress a true attractor pattern, John Alden Knight's colorful Mickey Finn. This is a sentimental favorite of mine, as it was the first fly I ever tied, but it is also a marvelously effective lure, in the appropriate setting. While essentially a wilderness-type dressing, the Mickey can be deadly in off-color water after a storm, and it is a super panfish, bass, and pickerel lure.

At first it might appear that this is an easier pattern to dress than the Golden Darter and should have preceded it in the lesson sequence. However, I think you will discover that working with deer tail can be quite a challenge, particularly for those who are concerned with neatness.

Mr. Knight's original pattern specifications call for a small bunch of yellow bucktail, topped by an equal bunch of red bucktail, over which is tied another bunch of yellow equal in thickness to the first two bunches combined. With due respect to the originator, I don't consider those proportions sacred and suggest you not get hung up on it. The most important factor is to maintain separation between the bunches, so that the red stripe is well defined.

I use the terms *bucktail* and *deer tail* interchangeably, as I am never really sure whether or not I am using the tail of a male deer. By the way, hairwing streamers are also referred to as *bucktails*, even when the hair is of some other type.

PATTERN DESCRIPTION

HOOK: Size 8, 6X long
THREAD: Black, pre-waxed
BODY: Medium flat silver tinsel
RIBBING: Medium oval silver tinsel
WING: Small bunch of yellow bucktail, topped by an equal bunch of red bucktail, and topped by another bunch of yellow bucktail somewhat thicker than the first.

TYING STEPS

1. Cover the hook with thread and tie in the oval ribbing tinsel just ahead of the bend, on the far side of the hook. Don't chop off the excess—bind it down to form a smooth underbody, working the thread forward to about ⅛ inch (3 mm) behind the eye, or a hair more.

2. Tie in a ten-inch (250 mm) piece of medium flat tinsel at the throat, silver side out. Secure with several tight wraps, and trim off the excess.

3. Start wrapping the tinsel rearward. The recommended technique is to partially overlap the previous turn, then pull the tinsel rearward at an angle, causing the wrap just taken to slide off the one before and lie neatly against the previous wrap. Avoid gaps where the thread shows through.

NOTE: Today's mylar tinsel is considerably thinner than the metallic tinsel of old. Thus, it does not slip off the previous wrap with as pronounced a click as the old stuff. As long as the body is coming out smooth, don't be too concerned if the wraps overlap a bit.

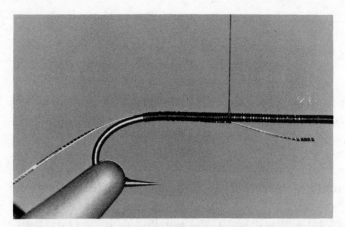

Ribbing tinsel in place, excess being bound down to form smooth under-body.

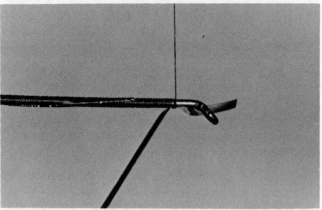

Tie in and secure flat tinsel here.

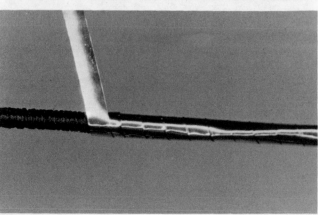

Flat tinsel being wrapped.

4. At the bend, start wrapping forward over the first layer of tinsel. Now it is more important that each wrap slips off the previous one. Still, if the body is smooth, a slight overlap is okay.

5. Tie off the tinsel at the throat with several tight wraps, then double the tinsel and lock it in with several more wraps. Trim off the excess.

6. Retrieve the ribbing tinsel and wind forward, keeping the spirals evenly spaced and not too close together. On this size hook, you should end up with seven or eight turns. Tie off at the throat.

NOTE: It is important that there *not* be a turn of ribbing tinsel passing over the top of the hook too close to where the wing will be tied on. If this occurs, back off a few turns and slightly adjust the spacing.

7. Create a thread base ⅛ inch (3 mm) in length, or a tiny bit more. Position the thread equidistant between the tinsel and the eye.

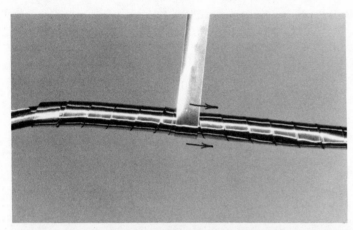

Coming back the other way.
Recommended method is to create slight overlap, then let tinsel slip forward to form neat, contiguous wraps.

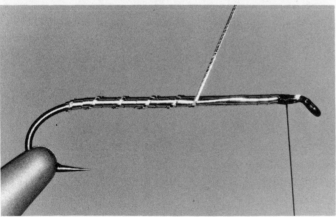

Wrapping the oval tinsel rib.
Note spacing.

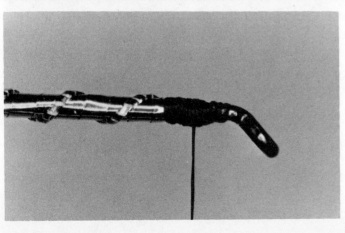

Prepare thread base for first layer of wing while tying off ribbing tinsel.

Before the next step, here are some planning instructions so that you may visualize the effect which is wanted, and how to obtain it. Several objectives are to be accomplished:
- Isolation of each bunch of hair, so that it doesn't mix with the one below it
- Tight, secure thread wraps, so that the fly stays together when cast and fished
- A neat, tapered head

To achieve this, we are going to "pyramid" the layers of thread, tapering the head as we go. The thread base is the first tier of the pyramid. The illustrations show how the three succeeding layers are constructed.

8. Cut off a bunch of yellow bucktail. Hold the tip end with the left hand, and stroke out the short hairs. Also remove any overly curly hairs and any hairs that appear reversed in the bunch— these are broken ends. Overly long hairs can be pulled out from the tip end and either discarded or laid back in the bunch, repositioned for proper length. The most common mistake in making bucktails is using too much hair. Observe the quantities in the photographs.

NOTE: I do not advocate the use of a hair-stacker for manicuring this type of wing, because the resulting silhouette is too abrupt in the rear. There are cases where I do use the stacker on streamer wings, but they are outside of the purview of this book.

9. Lay the bucktail atop the hook and adjust for proper length—1½ to 1¾ times the body length. Then tie on the bunch, taking care that the hairs stay on top of the hook.

10. Make tight wraps rearward to where the thread base ends and then forward to where the bunch was tied on.

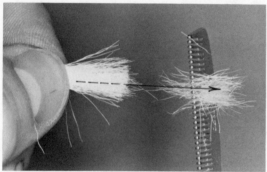

Clean out underfur and short hairs, either with fingers or fine-toothed comb.

Position first bunch of hair. Note length.

Tying on the hair.

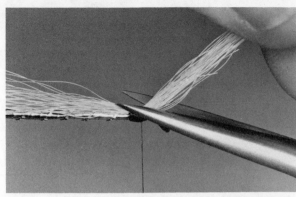

Trimming on bias.

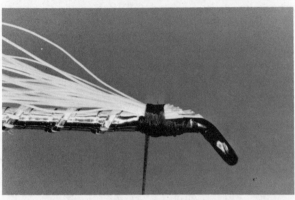

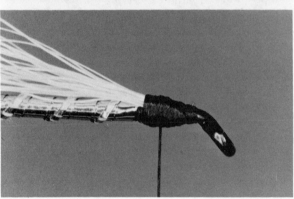

Thread positioned for tying on the second layer.

11. Cut off the butts on a slant. Then wrap forward to the eye and back—thus building the second tier of the pyramid. Position the thread a bit farther back than where the bunch was tied on.

12. Obtain a bunch of red bucktail equal in size to the yellow, and manicure as before. Tie it on at the thread position, and secure with tight wraps, working rearward, then forward to the tie-on point.

NOTE: Do not wrap the thread farther back than the rear extremity of the wraps that secure the first bunch. The key to maintaining separation is to tie hair over thread, not hair over hair.

Tying on and securing the second layer.

13. Trim the butts on a slant. Then wrap forward and back to bind down the trimmed ends, continuing to create the tapered head. Position the thread a bit farther back than where the red bunch was tied on.

14. Obtain another bunch of yellow bucktail somewhat thicker than the first one, and manicure it. Then tie it on at the thread position and secure with tight wraps rearward and forward, stopping at the tie-on point. Trim on a slant, continuing the head taper.

15. Wrap forward to the eye, then rearward over all previous wraps, then forward again, stopping a few turns short of the eye. Whip-finish and cement.

Second layer after trimming.
Note contour.

Thread position preparatory to tying on
third layer.

Third layer tied on. Note head shape
created by pyramid technique.

Wrapping thread at an angle as an aid
to forming head.

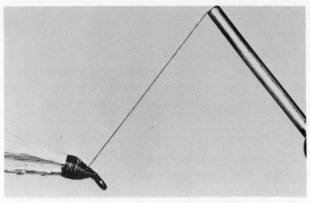

The completed fly.

NOTE: Sometimes it is difficult to wrap the tapered head without the thread slipping forward. One way to cope with this is to take some extra wraps at the front, thus reducing the severity of the slope. Another trick is to work the thread at an angle, as though trying to intersect the seven-o'clock and one-o'clock positions on a clock face.

Alternative method for keeping layers separated.

After tying enough of these flies to have developed a modicum of skill, test them by trying to pull out the red bunch. If it can be removed without real exertion, the fly was not properly constructed. We all like neat heads on our flies, but it is far more important that they don't come apart. Feel free to extend the thread base a bit and wrap over more of the hair. You can also put a small drop of cement between each layer, if you like.

Another technique which abets both tightness and separation is to take a turn of thread *around the hair itself,* then snug it down onto the thread base below. The other rules regarding positioning and tapering must still be observed. This is a bit tricky, and I suggest you develop your thread-management skills before incorporating this technique into your arsenal. I use it only on the second and third bunches, by the way.

Many hairwing streamers use only one color or type of hair, so separation is not an issue. Still, I prefer to pyramid several bunches of hair for tighter construction and better head-tapering. It is not good practice to tie a thick bunch of hair onto a hook because the entire center mass is held only by surrounding hair—and that's not sufficient to secure it, no matter how much thread pressure is applied. Be particularly attentive to this methodology when using slippery hairs such as squirrel tail and fitch tail.

A word about the selection of deer tails. I look for medium-size tails with the straightest hairs I can find—though even the straightest bucktail is slightly crinkly. I also like fine hair because most of my streamers are small. Very large bucktails are good for saltwater streamers and other big flies.

THE OPTIC HEAD

Are the heads on your streamers coming out oversized? There is a Chinese proverb which says, "When life gives you lemons, make lemonade." So, let us dress up our big-headed bucktails and turn them into objects of beauty.

Creating the optic effect simply means painting an eye on either side of the head. The first prerequisite is a head large enough to put eyes on, so you may wish to build yours up with additional thread.

In addition to clear head cement, you will need two colors of lacquer—yellow and black. Purchase the quick-drying type used by hobbyists. For ages, tyers have used Cellire, a famous and traditional product. It is slow-drying and messy, and there are definitely better lacquers available.

1. Coat the head with one even coat of clear head cement and then two coats of black lacquer.

2. Take a cylindrical object—a common kitchen match will do—and make a large yellow dot on either side of the head. Simply dip the end into the yellow lacquer and touch it to the head while holding the fly in a horizontal position. Do not use too much lacquer. After shaking the bottle to insure a thorough mix, the amount which sticks to the inside of the cap should be sufficient.

3. After the dots have dried, take a smaller cylindrical object, such as a cocktail toothpick cut in half, and make a black dot in the center of each yellow dot.

4. When the black dots have dried, finish off the head with a coat of clear lacquer.

Does the optic head contribute to a fly's effectiveness? I am positive that it does, at least in some areas. Steelheaders of the Pacific Northwest have favored optic patterns for decades. I was definitely able to identify a preference when fishing Alaska with streamers. It certainly dresses up one's fly box.

MYLAR TUBING AND CRAFT FUR

Synthetics are widely used in fly-tying today. While I don't like all of them, some are just great for making streamer wings. I particularly favor a product called craft fur, which can be obtained in most hobby shops at low cost. It is very easy to work with and has a translucency reminiscent of polar bear—a material at the heart of some environmental controversies.

Mylar tubing is of the same material as the tinsel we have been using. It is primarily used by clothing makers as decorative piping and can be obtained in fabric stores as well as fly-tying shops. It comes in several colors, including gold and silver, and also in several thicknesses, which accomodates various hook sizes and body-weighting techniques. Wrapping tinsel over a weighted body is a thankless task. Mylar tubing works much better.

Let's tie a Mickey Finn with a weighted body, using these materials.

PATTERN DESCRIPTION

HOOK: Size 6, 6X long (one size larger)
THREAD: Both black and white
BODY: Silver mylar tubing
UNDERBODY: Light-colored yarn, fine
WEIGHT: Fine lead wire
WINGS: Yellow and red craft fur

TYING STEPS

1. Using the black thread, tie on at the front, wrap to near the bend, and tie in an eight-inch (200 mm) piece of yarn. Let it repose in the materials clip, like ribbing tinsel.

2. Wind the thread forward to the throat. Then cut off a ten-inch (250 mm) piece of lead wire and wrap it per instructions in the Wooly Worm lesson. Remember, the thread is not involved—simply wind the lead around the hook. It should cover about seventy percent of the shank and should be centered. Coat with cement.

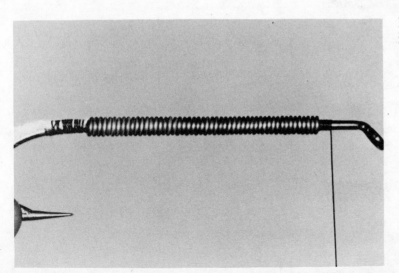

Lead wire underbody in place, yarn tied in at bend.

3. Wrap the yarn forward over the wire, using firm, contiguous wraps, and tie off at the throat.

4. Tie off the thread with a whip-finish or series of half-hitches.

5. Cut off a piece of silver mylar tubing the length of the shank and extract the fibre core with tweezers. The tubing should be in the neighborhood of 1/8 inch (3 mm) in diameter, or slightly less.

6. Slide the tubing over the underbody until the rear end of it reaches just beyond the bend.

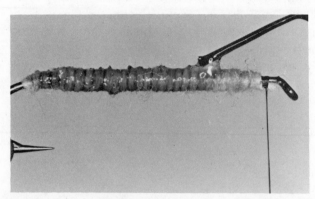

Yarn wrapped, cement being applied.

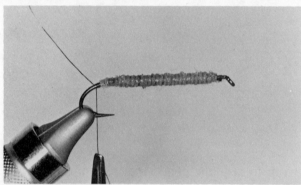

Re-affixing tying thread at rear of hook.

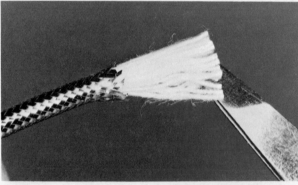

Removing core from Mylar-tubing.

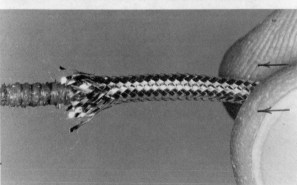

Sliding tubing over underbody.

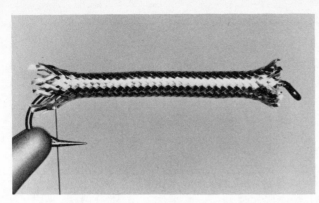

Tubing in place.

7. Using white thread, tie on over the tag ends of the mylar and bind them down firmly. Trim the mylar, then tie off with a whip-finish, using a slightly larger loop than you would for a head knot.

8. Tie on again with the black thread, binding down the front ends of the mylar in the process. The tag ends may tend to separate, so be sure you don't miss any. Trim, then neaten up the area with some discreet thread wraps, creating a base for the wings.

9. Construct the wings, using yellow-red-yellow bunches of craft fur, just as you did the deer tail. Don't use your fine scissors to cut off the craft fur; it's a bit tough for them. Before tying on the bunches, pull out the underfur, as you did with the short hairs of the deer tail.

Securing tubing at bend. Trim off
excess tubing, then make a
whip finish here and coat with cement.

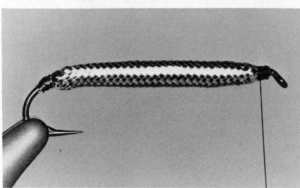

Tie on again at the front, securing
the forward end of the tubing in
the process.

Three-layer wing in place, head built up
to accommodate optic effect.

10. Finish off the head, and whip-finish. Before applying cement, make a couple of passes through the wing with a fine-tooth comb. Surprisingly, this will not cause the bunches to mix—it will separate the fibers, improving the fly's appearance and action. Then cement both the head and butt thread wraps. Lift the wing when cementing the butt.

First layer of eye, a dot of yellow lacquer.

Pupil of eye, a dot of black lacquer.

A few closing words about mylar tubing are in order here. I'm sure you have noticed that it is similar to a Chinese finger cuff in construction. This allows adjustment of both length and diameter, so that an absolutely precise match with the thickness of the underbody isn't necessary. Ideally, the tubing should fit snugly over the underbody. If it seems a bit loose, compress it by pushing it forward with the left hand before tying the front end down.

If your underbody seems a bit thick for the tubing—don't despair—the tubing will expand like a snake eating its dinner. Use a slightly longer piece, as length will be sacrificed for diameter. Don't try to pull the tubing over the body from the rear, as the finger-cuff phenomenon will cause it to tighten. Push from the front, then pull, then push again until the tubing is in place. This contraction-expansion process is called *caging*. Braided-butt leaders are worked onto a fly line in the same manner.

This pattern lesson completes our studies of subsurface fly construction. The best has been saved for last. Let's move upward to the realm of the dry fly.

16

THE DUN VARIANT

TECHNIQUES TO BE LEARNED

1. Basic dry-fly concepts
2. Dry-fly tail
3. Stripped-hackle-quill body
4. Dry-fly hackle

This pattern is one of three variant-type dressings found in Art Flick's little gem of a book, *New Streamside Guide to Naturals and Their Imitations*. It is more than simply a pattern—it is a unique design, as well. It features oversize hackles, a long tail, and a wingless design. The hackle color matches the slate wings of the family of mayflies that Art sought to simulate—it is obvious that a credible wing impression was part of the design criteria. Variants are high floaters, an important attribute in the tumbling freestone streams Art loved to fish.

I believe the variant style to be a good starting point for the developing dry-fly tyer. It is simple enough—there are only three components—and the absence of wings removes a major stumbling block for novice tyers. Dry-fly wings aren't really difficult to tie, but they do require a bit of practice.

The dressing in Art's book specifes a short-shank hook. I use a regular dry-fly hook for simplicity.

PATTERN DESCRIPTION

HOOK: Size 14 dry fly, typically a Mustad 94840
THREAD: Black
TAIL: Long, stiff slate-colored hackle barbules
BODY: The center quill of a large brown hackle, cape or saddle, the darker the better
HACKLE: Two slate-dun rooster cape feathers
NOTE: It is desirable to strip the body quills a day ahead of time and soak them overnight in water.

TYING STEPS

1. Tie on in the middle of the hook, and wrap to the bend.

2. Make a little bump of thread right where the bend begins—this will help spread the tails.

3. For tail material, try to find a large, stiff-barbed feather around the edges of a cape. If none are present, use a large hackle feather from elsewhere on the cape. Gather a bunch of barbules from the stem near the tip, where they are the stiffest. About a dozen barbules is adequate.

NOTE: You will notice a webbed area which runs along either side of the center quill. When tying dry-fly tails, be sure the web is covered by the thread, thus becoming part of the underbody. Only the stiff portion of the fibres is suitable for tailing.

4. Variant tails should be long, about *twice* the shank length. With the left thumb and forefinger, mount the bunch atop the hook and tie it down with a pinch, about two or three wraps from the bump.

5. Secure the tail with a couple of firm wraps to the rear, forcing the barbules against the thread bump. When they spread, work forward a few turns, and then trim the excess, cutting on a taper, where the thread was originally tied on. Continue wrapping forward to the tie-on point and back to the bend, forming an underbody.

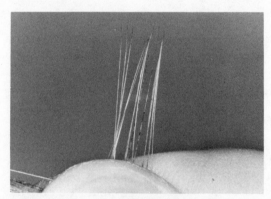

Isolating a bunch of long, stiff barbules for the tail. Note evened-up tips.

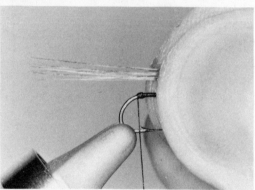

The Variant tail is longer than the standard dry-fly tail.
Note thread bump.

Tail tied on. Note spread in top view.

6. The body quill is prepared by stripping the barbules from both sides. As stated, it is best to do this a day ahead of time, so the quill can become well soaked and pliant. Typically, the middle third of the quill will form the body on a variant of this size, so trim off the first inch or so of the tip.

7. Tie in the thin end of the quill at the bend, and secure with a few firm wraps. Then trim the excess on an angle at the front of the underbody and bind down with firm, contiguous wraps.

8. Wrap the quill, applying moderate tension, each turn abutting the previous one.

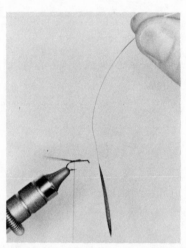

The stripped quill.

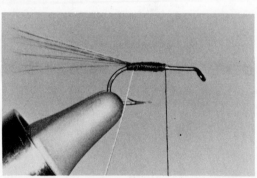

Underbody formed, quill tied in at base of tail.

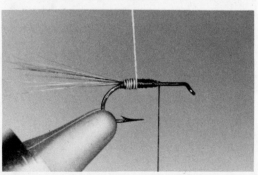

Quill being wrapped.

9. When the front of the underbody is reached, take a half-turn more, then bind down the excess quill along the bottom of the hook shank with firm, neat wraps, working forward into the area where the hackle will be wound.

10. Before getting too close to the eye, cut off the excess quill on a taper. Then wrap almost to the eye and back to the front of the body.

NOTE: At this juncture, I will explain the rationale underlying my rather stringent instructions. One of the worst situations, when hackling a dry fly, is to be forced to wrap the hackles over a bumpy surface. Had we stubbed off the excess quill, there would have been a "step" at that point—thus, we ran it forward almost to the eye. While we do not want to build up bulk, a neat extra layer of thread is preferable to an uneven base for the hackles.

11. The hackles on a variant are about two sizes larger than normal. In other words, a size 14 hook gets size 10 hackles. If you have a hackle gauge, refer to it for sizing. If not, you can estimate. A size 10 hackle is 2½ to 3 times the gape of a size 14 hook, or just over ½ inch (13 mm) from center quill to barbule tips.

Two matching hackles.

Approximate length of useable hackle.
This varies from feather to feather.

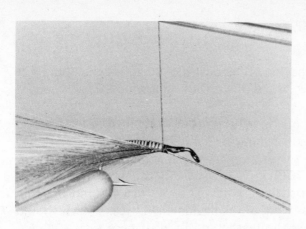

Hackle tie-in. Note how thread
has been applied to area
where hackle will be wrapped.

12. Select two hackle feathers and pull them from the cape. They will be long, probably about five inches (125 mm). Only about the outer ⅓ will actually be used in the hackling process, so cut them in half and strip the barbules from the stem until a point is reached where center web is minimal and the barbules are relatively stiff and shiny. The proportions will vary slightly from cape to cape, of course.

13. Tie in the hackle feathers together, holding them standing on edge beneath the hook shank in the position shown in the illustration. Leave the tiniest bit of stem exposed, so that the feathers will be in the winding attitude when the first barbules begin to deploy.

NOTE: There has been some debate over the years as to whether hackles should be tied in with the shiny sides facing forward, rearward, or one facing each way. Given decent-quality hackle, you needn't worry about this, as the end result will be the same—so, suit yourself.

14. Bind down the stems with neat, firm wraps. Well before the eye, cut off the butts on an angle. Wrap forward to the eye, then back three turns, thus creating space for tying off the hackles and doing the whip-finish.

15. Grasp one of the feathers with your hackle pliers, taking care to seize enough stem to avoid slipping or breakage. Tension is gentle, but firm and constant.

16. Make the first turn just forward of the body. The technique is the same as for the wet flies we hackled in previous chapters. Pass the pliers over with the left hand, and catch them coming under with the right hand—each wrap contiguous to the previous one. How many turns you will get is hard to say—it depends on the properties of the feather. Five to seven is typical. Don't try to squeeze out every last turn—you may crowd the eye. Also, keep in mind that the barbules near the tip get shorter, meaning that they create congestion without contributing proportionately to the floatation of the fly.

Left: Preparatory position which
sets up first turn of hackle.

Right: First hackle being wound.

17. When the thread position is reached, tie the hackle off against the far side of the hook. Let the bobbin hang, maintaining tension, while the tip is bound down with tight wraps. Try to keep it from rolling around into the throat area.

18. When you are sure the tip is secured, trim it off by pulling it out straight from the far side of the hook and clipping it, while the thread hangs suspended. If there are any stray barbules around the eye, pull them off to one side, either with your fingers or hackle pliers, and clip them.

19. Wind the second hackle as you did the first. If there is any space between the front of the body and the previously applied hackle, take the first turn there. You will usually find that the second hackle melds readily into the first, without skewing or displacing any fibres. If such should occur, back off a turn and try again, slightly altering the feather position, if necessary.

20. Tie off the second hackle as you did the first. Police the area, disposing of any stray barbules.

21. Secure with a few more tight wraps, then whip-finish. Cement both the head and body. The quill requires two coats for adequate protection, and don't neglect the underside.

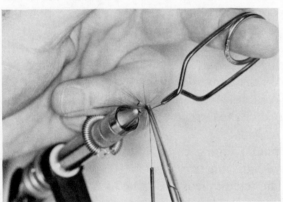

Trimming excess. Note how hackle pliers are used to keep material clear of eye.

Second hackle being wound over and through first hackle.

The completed fly.

ABOUT QUILLS

The stripped-hackle-quill body is called for on a number of superb patterns, notably the Red Quill and the other two variants in Art Flick's book, the Cream and the Grey Fox. Feathers of various colors are used, in order to obtain the desired effect. While natural colors are favored, these quills can be tinted, when the shade one wants isn't at hand.

There are two methods of doing this: a regular dye bath or touching up with a felt marker. The latter is easier, but you may find that the thinner in the head cement interacts with the ink when the protective body coating is applied. Using a top-quality marker is helpful—I particularly recommend the Pantone brand. Dab on the body coating carefully, let the first coat dry thoroughly, and you should be okay.

If you anticipate doing a lot of these bodies over a period of time, I suggest you strip a large batch of quills some cold winter afternoon and put them in storage. An olive bottle full of water will do, but better results are obtained by adding a little creme hair rinse such as Tame. A fifteen to twenty percent solution is about right. This softens the quills so that they don't split when being wrapped. The pliability of a quill can be deceiving. Often a dry quill will tolerate being wrapped without splitting, only to break loose and unwind itself later. Goodbye fly.

Some dealers sell stripped saddle-hackle quills in bundles, saving the tyer much labor. Almost invariably, these come from ginger or light brown saddles, making them appropriate for the Grey Fox Variant and the Red Quill. Tinting is generally required for the Dun Variant, where a darker brown is wanted.

17

THE FOXY QUILL

TECHNIQUES TO BE LEARNED

1. The wood-duck wing (teal substitute)
2. The peacock quill body
3. Mixing hackle

This is a concoction I put together a few years ago while searching for ways to reduce the number of patterns in my fly box. It combines the better features of several outstanding patterns—the body of the Quill Gordon, the wing coloration of the Adams, and the hackle mixture of the Grey Fox. I have used it with great success during various insect hatches and as an attractor. I tie it in sizes 8 through 16.

Beyond being a great fish-taker, the Foxy Quill is also an ideal "teaching" fly. The Peacock quill body is used on several major patterns, and the flank-feather wing is probably the most widely employed of all dry-fly winging methods. Wood-duck flank reigns supreme, adorning such classics as the Quill Gordon, Hendrickson, and Light Cahill. Its lemon-barred shade is beautiful indeed, and its texture makes it the most pleasing to use of all the flank feathers. For this pattern we shall use teal, also a nice feather to work with, and far less expensive than wood duck.

PATTERN DESCRIPTION

HOOK: Dry fly, size 12
THREAD: Yellow, beige, or white
TAIL: Straw cream and grizzly mixed, or either by itself
BODY: Stripped quill from the eye of a peacock tail
WINGS: Barred teal flank feather, or mallard substitute
HACKLE: Straw cream and grizzly, one of each
NOTE: True straw cream hackle is not always easy to obtain. Feel free to substitute light ginger.

TYING STEPS

1. Tie on a short distance in back of the eye and wrap evenly and neatly to the midpoint of the shank, then forward to a point about ⅓ of the shank length from the eye.

2. Select a teal flank feather which has a symmetrical, nicely formed tip. Strip off the waste fibres down toward the butt on either side of the center quill until the feather is about ¾ of an inch (18 mm) wide across the tip.

3. Hold the feather with the left thumb and forefinger near the base, gripping the lower twenty-five percent. Then fold the fibres on either side of the center quill with a downward stroke of the right thumb and forefinger.

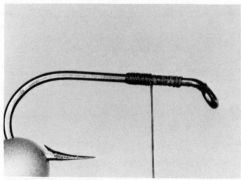

Preparation of thread base for tie-in of wing material.

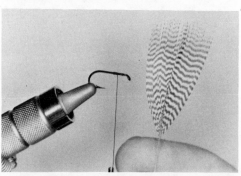

Teal flank feather, center portion.

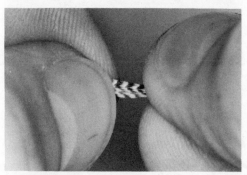

Fold the feather tip, forming two layers.

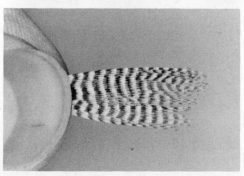

4. Re-grip the feather near the base in its folded position with the left thumb and forefinger.

5. Compact the fibres into a tight bunch by pinching them with the right thumb and forefinger.

6. Re-grip the feather in its compacted position with the left thumb and forefinger. You now have it properly prepared for tying on. The idea is to get all of the tip ends fairly even.

7. The wing should be equal to the shank length of the hook, or perhaps a bit longer. Measure, then mount the feather atop the shank so that the first wrap of thread will permanently establish the wing length.

8. Tie on the wing feather, using the pinch. Make three firm wraps rearward and then three more coming forward again to the point where the feather was tied on.

9. Observe to see that the fibres have remained on top of the hook—this is *very* important. If they have slipped down around the sides, pull them back up on top by preening the entire bunch upward. If they resist, back off the thread a wrap or two. When you have the bunch set nicely on top of the hook, lock it in with several tight wraps back and forth.

10. Trim the butt portion of the feather on an elongated taper, extending almost to the bend. This will contribute to the shaping of the body.

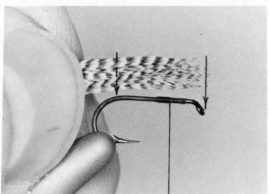

Length of wing is approximately that of hook shank from bend to eye.

Tie on wing feather, using the pinch.

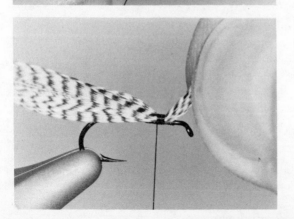

Before totally securing wing, be sure all fibres are on top of the hook.

11. Next, we will stand the bunch upright and lock it in position with a few turns of thread. It is important to absolutely minimize the number of thread wraps required, so as to avoid creating a large lump, which will interfere with winding the hackle later on. Thus, we hold the feathers up with the left hand and crimp them with the right thumb.

12. When the bunch is well-crimped and almost stands up on its own, lock it in place with several wraps tight to the base, working back against the tie-on point.

Crimp fibres with thumb so that they tend to stand up by themselves.

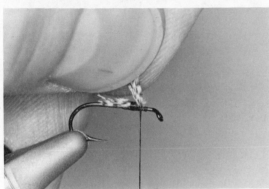

Hold fibres erect and secure with wraps tight to base of wing.

13. We will now divide and secure the wings. A wordy narrative is of little value here. Simply follow the pictures and captions.

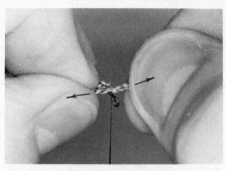

Divide fibres into two equal bunches and spread with fingers.

The wings are secured in the divided position with an "X" or criss-cross of thread. Step 1: bring thread directly upward, ahead of near-side wing.

Step 2: pass thread through the notch and down behind far-side wing.

Step 3: pass thread beneath hook and up behind near-side wing.

Step 4: pass thread through notch and downward in front of far-side wing. This completes the "X".

The wings are secured in position with the figure-8 technique. Begin as you would the "X", passing the thread through the notch to a position behind the far-side wing. Then seize the far-side wing firmly with your left thumb and forefinger.

While maintaining your grip, make a snug turn of thread around the very base of the wing.

Continue the wrap back through the notch, so that it has passed completely around the base of the far-side wing. Maintain grip on wing until the thread is hanging straight down behind the near-side wing, with the weight of the bobbin supported essentially by the hook shank. Now you may release the wing.

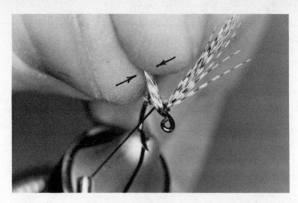

Seize the near-side wing firmly with the left thumb and forefinger and begin to make a snug turn around the very base of the near-side wing.

Bring the thread around in back of the wing, then forward through the notch and straight down on the far side of the hook in back of the far-side wing. Keep the thread tight to the wing base at all times. This completes the figure 8. You will probably want to make a second one, to ensure that the wing will remain in position for the life of the fly.

Note that the excess wing material has been trimmed on an accentuated taper. Bind it down, forming the underbody.

14. Having completed the wings, wrap the thread to the bend to bind down the underbody. Then make a tail as you did on the Dun Variant, but not as long—the shank length, or perhaps a bit more, will suffice. Remember to make the little thread bump to spread the fibres. If using the mixed cream and grizzly—which I prefer—cut off two equal bunches of fibres, even up the tips, and roll them between the right thumb and forefinger to effect the mixing. Trim the excess just behind the wings.

Tail in place, peacock quill tied in, dark edge to the rear.

15. We will now prepare the body quill. Select a frond from the eyed portion of a peacock tail feather—refer to "About Peacock Eyes," following these tying instructions. Lay it flat on a piece of cardboard. Hold down the skinny end, and rub off the herl using the "ink" end of an ink/pencil eraser. Do both sides, working toward the butt.

16. When all herl has been cleaned off, you will have a tapered quill with a light and dark edge. Given a good-sized, mature eye, the quill will be close to two inches (50 mm) in length. The very slender portion at the tip is weak and poorly marked, and will not be used. Tie on the quill with the dark edge to the rear, holding it flat atop the hook with the left thumb and passing the thread over the top.

17. Bind down the excess quill with neat, contiguous wraps, working forward to a point just behind the wings, then trim the excess.

18. A delicate touch is required when wrapping the body quill. You may use your fingers—but I do better with hackle pliers. The first wrap is taken right at the base of the tail. The dark edge remains rearward so that a light/dark segmentation is created with each succeeding turn. The wraps should abut neatly.

19. Space must be allocated for hackle behind the wings—so stop the body one full quill width shy of the wings. Tie off the quill on the bottom of the hook. When you trim, let a stub extend forward under the thorax, almost to the eye. This contributes to the creation of a smooth surface over which to wind hackle and also locks in the quill.

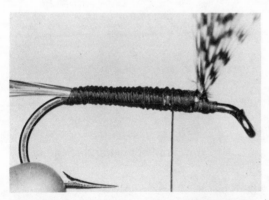

Note gentle taper of underbody, also thread position.

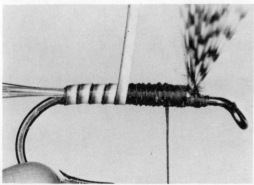

Quill being wound. Note light/dark segmentation.

20. Select one straw-colored and one grizzly hackle of equal barbule length. This is determined by flexing the feathers to simulate the winding attitude. These hackles will be normal size for a number 12 hook, which means they will have about a 7/16 inch (10 mm) radius when wound. Strip back to the quality portion of the feathers and tie them in together, beneath the shank, standing on edge, just behind the wings.

21. Secure the stems with several tight wraps behind the wings, then continue forward, creating as smooth a base as possible. You are also binding down that little stub of body quill.

22. Trim off the stems, leaving sufficient space to tie off the hackles and make the whip-finish. Bind down the stubs and police the area with a few discreet wraps.

23. Now for winding the hackle—first, inspect the two feathers. If one is shorter, wind it first so it will have the advantage of encircling the smallest possible diameter.

24. Make two turns behind the wing. Then cross over beneath the thorax and make the next turn tight to the base of the wing, in front. Several more turns will bring you to where you left the thread. Tie off the hackle and trim, disposing of stray fibers, as you did with the Dun Variant.

25. Follow suit with the second hackle.

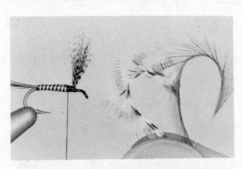

Sizing the hackles.
Note space between front of body and wing on completed body.

Hackle feathers tied in on bottom of hook behind wing, stems trimmed off, area prepared for winding of hackle, first hackle in starting-to-wind position.
Note thread position.

Left: Hackle is wound both behind and ahead of wings.

Right: Second hackle is also wound behind and ahead of wings.

The completed fly. Protect the quill with two coats of cement.

NOTE: The number of turns specified behind and in front of the wing are benchmarks. The number actually obtained will depend on precisely how you have positioned the components of the fly and, to a degree, on the hackles themselves.

26. Whip-finish, and cement head and body.

ABOUT PEACOCK EYES

The colorful-eyed portion of a peacock tail feather is unique in that the stripped quills manifest the light/dark contrast so desirable in making segmented bodies. Sometimes, a little contrast is present in quills from the stem proper, but I've yet to see one I would use for the type of body we just constructed.

The amount of contrast varies between feathers. Observe the back sides. Squeeze the fibers and look for a flash of light coloration. Usually, the larger, more mature eyes have the best contrast—and of course, the quills are longer, stronger, and easier to work with. They cost more, but it's worth the difference when one considers the number of quills obtained from one prime eye.

Peacock feathers sometimes become matted and crushed from transport and storage. They can be quickly restored by steaming.

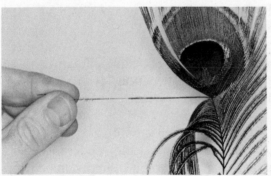

Eye area of peacock plume where quills having light/dark contrast are found.

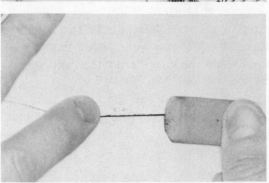

Removing herl with eraser.

ABOUT FLANK FEATHERS

It is often possible to make two or even three pair of wings out of one flank feather, depending upon its size and shape and the size of fly being dressed. Do we care? Yes, for two reasons:
- A fly with excess material in the wings is poorly balanced.
- If the flank feather is wood duck, it is valuable, and not always readily available. Thus, optimum utilization should be made of each feather.

Let's examine a large, prime wood duck feather, after stripping off the waste material near the butt. Notice that it can be separated into three sections—the tip fibres and one on each side of the center quill. Obviously, the tip lends itself readily to being folded, bunched, and made into wings, as we learned in the pattern lesson. Either or both of the side sections are also usable on a decent-quality feather.

A prime wood-duck flank feather,
with potential for winging three flies.

Sometimes the side sections lack sufficient fibres to be used individually, but can be made into handsome wings when combined. This is done as follows:
1. Stroke the fibers outward from the stem so that the tips become even.
2. Carefully cut each section from the stem. Notice that they have opposing curvature.
3. Face the two convex sides together, keeping the tips of the two sections even.
4. Compact the sections so that they become bunches. They are now ready to be tied on and formed into wings.

When forming wings out of a single bunch, I first assess how much curvature exists. If the curvature is significant, I fold the bunch in half, convex side to convex side, and proceed in accordance with the instructions just given. If the curvature is negligible, I simply bunch the fibres, tie them on, and let the thread maneuvers take care of the rest.

Mallard and teal flanks are commonly dyed the approximate color of wood duck. The resulting product isn't the equal of the real thing, but given a proper dye job and well-graded feathers, it can be quite acceptable. I particularly recommend imitation wood duck to the novice, who will be using up material while perfecting his or her technique.

I used the term *well-graded feathers*. By this, I mean ones which have the shape and markings which lend themselves to wing-making, and which bear some resemblance to natural wood duck.

Usually, such grading must be done by the tyer, as feathers are dyed in bulk quantities by the dealers and distributors. You will find that a lot of the flank feathers from teal and mallards aren't good winging material. The percentage of usable feathers is much higher with real wood duck.

It's quite practical to do your own dye job. Simply obtain some Veniard Summer Duck dye and follow the instructions in the package. I suggest you pre-sort the feathers—why dye up a batch and end by throwing half of it away? For best results, wash the feathers first using regular liquid dishwashing detergent and rinse thoroughly. You needn't wait for them to dry—in fact, it's better if you don't.

18

THE BLUE-WINGED OLIVE

TECHNIQUES TO BE LEARNED

1. Tippet wing, shaped with wing burners or trimmed
2. Clean-silhouette dry-fly-style dubbing

A great many important mayflies have wings of grey, ranging in shade from pale watery grey to charcoal. Several types of materials have been used to imitate these wings on dry flies, including quill sections from the wings of various birds, an assortment of animal hairs, small hackle tippets, and most recently, synthetic yarns and fabrics.

Of them all, I favor hackle tippets for most applications. They are easy to work with, readily available, delicate yet sturdy, and come in a full range of realistic shades. They are adaptable to virtually any hook size, including the small ones where bulkier materials simply don't work. While I feel that synthetics have great possibilities, I am very partial to hackle tippets when a delicate fly with a clean silhouette is desired.

From a functional standpoint, the most important factor in tippet wings is that they not twist the leader during casting. The feathers must be soft and the center quills fine. Also, the wings must be uniform in size and shape and must set squarely atop the hook. Thus, material selection and technique are both critical.

It's hard to equal a nice hen cape as a source of wing material. The feathers have soft barbules and stems, and the webby centers provide ideal density and opaqueness. Good hen capes aren't easy to find, particularly in natural dun shades. Dyed capes are okay, given a realistic-looking dye job.

Poor-quality rooster hackle can also be used successfully in making tippet wings. The very property which renders feathers unsuitable for hackling dry flies makes them desirable for wings: lots of web. You might keep this in mind when sorting through capes in the never-ending quest for hackle.

We will use a size 14 hook for this lesson. In the Northeast, where I do most of my fishing, the various flies we seek to imitate with this pattern rarely exceed a size 14. In fact, many of them run to a 16 or smaller. In the Rockies, there are several large blue-winged and olive-bodied flies which run to a size 8, or even larger. On the other end of the scale, there are tiny blue-winged olives which range from a size 20 all the way down to a size 28. Body and wing shadings vary widely, as several families and genera of mayflies produce blue-winged olives. It is a most interesting fly pattern, and of great importance to the angler.

PATTERN DESCRIPTION

HOOK: Dry fly, size 14
THREAD: Olive or white
WINGS: Grey (dun) hen hackles
TAIL: Grey (dun) barbules
BODY: Olive dubbing, very soft, natural or synthetic
HACKLE: Grey (dun)

TYING INSTRUCTIONS

1. Tie on a little way behind the eye, and create a thread base for mounting the wings by wrapping back to the middle of the shank and then forward to a point approximately thirty percent rearward of the eye.

2. Select two webby hen hackles. They should be of sufficient size that the shaped wings can be formed totally out of the web in the center.

Let's do wing burners here, and save trimming for later treatment as an option. First, examine the burners, and note that they are asymmetrical. This is because the designer wanted to effect a more realistic leading-edge/trailing-edge shape. It would be simpler if they were symmetrical, as we could then prepare both wings simultaneously without worrying about how they would match up later. As it stands, we can either burn the wings individually or both at once by facing them cupped side to cupped side. The choice is yours. I burn mine simultaneously.

Hen feathers suitable for this type of wing.

Feather mounted in wing-burner.

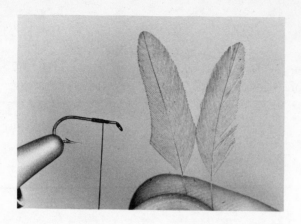

Feathers after being shaped by burning.

3. Strip the waste material near the butts, but leave the feathers long. Face the cupped sides together, with the tips even and the stems perfectly aligned.

4. Insert the feathers into a medium-size wing burner so that only the very tip of the webby area protrudes. Be sure stem alignment is maintained, so that the finished wings are mirror images of each other.

5. With a butane lighter or alcohol burner, singe off all of the excess material which sticks out around the perimeter of the wing burner. Then extract the wings and preen them a bit to remove the little nodules left by the flame.

6. Re-match the feathers convex side to convex side with the tips perfectly even. Note that they are much longer than needed. A word of explanation is in order here. I advocate not stripping off the excess material, because it gives the tyer something substantial to grip. It is much easier to handle feathered stems than bare ones, and it helps prevent them from rolling, which results in cocked wings and twisted leaders.

7. Gauge proper wing length. I like them to be slightly longer than the shank. Example: If the shank is ⅜ inches (9 to 10 mm), I make the wings ⁷⁄₁₆ inches (11 mm).

8. At the precise point where the thread must intersect the stems to establish the desired wing length, preen back the barbules, exposing the stems.

9. With the left thumb and forefinger, set the feathers atop the hook, so positioned that the first wrap of thread will pass over the stems at the exposed point.

10. Tie on the wings with a pinch, or perhaps two. Then lock them in with several firm wraps, working rearward and then forward again. Don't trim off the butts yet—there is always the possibility that the wings are not positioned properly, and you will have to repeat the process.

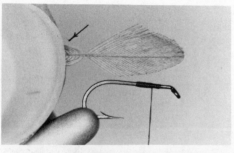

Gauge length relative to shank.
Note how excess material is gripped
by left thumb and forefinger.

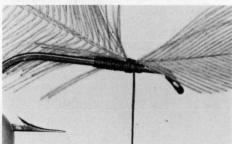

Wings in place.

11. Stand the wings up, using the left thumb and forefinger, then lock them in position with two or three wraps in front, tight against the base. Observe to see that they are not crooked or twisted. If the wings are crooked, unwrap the thread and re-tie them, or try to reposition them with some gentle manipulation.

NOTE: When the wings are stroked into the upright position, you may notice that the lowest barbule on each wing separates from the rest and pops out straight. Trim them off.

Securing wings in upright position.

12. When satisfied that the wings are on straight, trim off the waste material. Then wrap the thread rearward to the bend.

13. Make a tail out of a small bunch of grey barbules, using the techniques learned in the Foxy Quill pattern lesson. Bind down the butts, wrapping forward to where the body will end and then back nearly to the bend. Trim any excess butt material. Do not work into the area just behind the wings, where the hackle will be wound.

14. We will now construct a dubbed body, using the single-thread method. I re-emphasize: use soft, fine-textured material. Spin it onto the thread in very small wisps—you will be amazed at how little is required. Pack it tight, smooth, and thin, using a bit of supplementary wax on the thread, if you choose. A 1½-inch (37 mm) length is sufficient. Study the photograph.

NOTE: You will recall from earlier pattern lessons that it is difficult to apply dubbing right up against the hook. There are two ways to cope with this: either leave room for a few wraps of bare thread, working back toward the base of the tail, or position the thread at the bend and slide the dubbing up the thread until it meets the hook. This you can do when using the single-thread method.

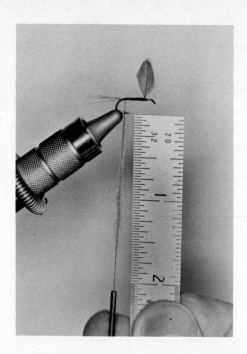

Dubbing should be thin.

15. Wrap the dubbed body, re-packing en route, if necessary. Stop when the space reserved for hackle is reached. It is poor practice to wind hackle over the front of the body.

16. If you have a really good-quality dun cape, one feather will provide sufficient hackle. With average-quality capes, two are generally required, as only the end portions are usable. Select one feather or two, as appropriate, and gauge for size. The radius, or barbule length, of size 14 hackle is about ⅜ inches (9 mm).

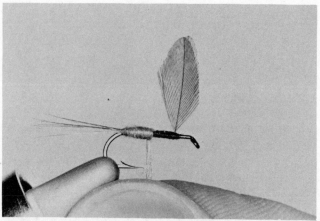

Dubbing being applied. Repack if necessary, as shown.

Body in place.

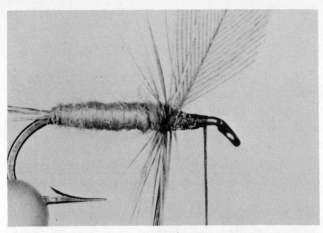

Hackle in progress. It is okay to tip the wing forward a bit while winding hackle behind it, provided no turns are taken against the base.

Restore wing to upright position and lock in place with hackle.

The completed fly.

17. If using a single feather, take two or three turns behind the wing, then cross over at the thorax and take the next turn in front of the wing, tight to the base, thus locking the wing into position. Finish off with several more turns. If using two feathers, take one or two turns behind the wing with each one, but take care not to lay one of the stems against the back of the wing, as this will cock it forward. Lock in the wing with a turn tight to the front with either or both of the hackles.

18. Trim, whip-finish, and cement. If white thread was used, touch up the head with an olive or brown marker.

If you don't have wing burners, shaped wings may be fashioned by trimming, either with scissors or nail clippers. The criteria are the same, in that the wings must be of uniform size and shape. The easiest way to ensure uniformity is to do both wings at once, as was illustrated with the wing burners. Again, be sure the stems are aligned. I recommend the stems also be centered. Later on, you can experiment with ultra-realistic sculptured effects, if you wish.

If you opt for nail clippers, they should be well made and sharp; otherwise they simply won't do the job. Toenail clippers seem to work the best.

Possibly you have seen demonstrations, either live or in print, where the tyer strips the stems bare before tying on the wings. I'm not saying this is wrong—I did it that way for years. Eventually it occurred to me that leaving the barbules on the stems would make for easier handling. I experimented with the Adams wings, which are made of intact, untrimmed grizzly hackle tippets. Immediately, my results improved—there was no more rolling and twisting—and I wasn't losing my hold, as I frequently did when handling the bare stems.

The only disadvantage with my unstripped method is that a little more bulk is developed behind the wings, due to the binding down of the barbules as well as the stems. This is minimal, and not a problem on average-size flies. On tiny drys, you may wish to employ the stripped-stem method. Here's how it's done:

1. Shape the tippets first. Then carefully pull off the barbules on each side of the quill until only that portion which will comprise the wings remains.

2. Grasp the feathers with the right thumb and forefinger, keeping the tips even. Position them atop the hook.

3. Seize the stems with the left hand, hold them against the top of the hook, and execute a pinch, with the thread intersecting the stems precisely at the base of the wings.

4. Secure them with perhaps a half-dozen wraps, and then stand the wings up as previously instructed. If they are twisted, repeat the process using slightly less thread tension, so that when the wings are stroked into the upright position, the stems can readjust a bit, and the twisting correct itself.

19

AN EASY HAIRWING CADDIS

TECHNIQUES TO BE LEARNED

1. Selecting, handling, and trimming deer-like hair
2. Palmered dry-fly hackle
3. The caddis silhouette—three variations

Since the dawn of fly-fishing, the mayfly has been the darling of the angler and tyer. This is understandable, as mayflies are considerably more distinctive in appearance than other stream insects we encounter, and therefore easier for the casual fisherman to relate to. Their striking contrasts in size and coloration have earned them famous names—Quill Gordon, March Brown, Leadwinged Coachman, Light Cahill, Sulphur Dun—the list goes on. Even the novice can probably identify a Green Drake on sight.

Not so with caddisflies. Only the most scientifically oriented members of the fly-fishing community can identify these insects accurately, and nicknames are virtually nonexistent. Generally, the hatches are referred to simply by size and color—big brown caddis, little tan caddis, jumping grey caddis, tiny black caddis. This, despite the fact that on many streams caddisflies are more plentiful and important than mayflies, and are almost as individualistic when examined closely.

The most obvious distinction between caddisflies and mayflies is the wing silhouette. Mayflies carry their wings more or less upright, whereas caddisflies carry their wings in tent-like, almost mothlike, fashion. Caddis wings are proportionately larger, compared to the body, than with comparably sized mayflies.

There are other striking differences between mayflies and caddisflies which are well documented in other publications, and will not be addressed here. However, there is one behavioral characteristic which deserves mention, as it has a bearing on how we design and tie our flies. This has to do with movement. Certain caddis are very active on the water—they jump, hop, and make abortive departures. It is sometimes maddening to try to simulate these movements, but often we can do so effectively by twitching or skipping our flies on the surface. This is why we resort to unique fly designs and buoyant materials for caddis imitations. One of the most popular is the hair of deer and deer-like animals.

We will talk further about deer and similar hairs after the pattern lesson. Now, let's learn to tie three versions of the Hairwing Caddis.

PATTERN DESCRIPTION, NO-HACKLE VERSION

HOOK: Dry fly, size 14
THREAD: Brown or black
BODY: Greyish-brown dubbing, natural or synthetic
WINGS/LEGS: Elk or deer body hair—grey, brown, or greyish-brown

TYING STEPS

1. Tie on near the front and wrap to the bend.

2. Make a dubbed body, using whatever material and method you prefer. Stop about twenty percent to the rear of the eye.

NOTE: Caddis bodies needn't be tapered in the same manner as mayfly bodies—a plain cylindrical shape will do. Actually, some of the natural insects are slightly thicker at the posterior.

3. Select a bunch of short, grey or greyish-brown body hair, either deer or elk. By short, I mean 1¼ to 1½ inches (32–40 mm) in length. The bunch should be approximately the thickness of a pencil. This will be greatly reduced by the manicuring process.

4. Hold the bunch by the tip end and strip out all of the underfur and short hairs.

5. A hair stacker is of great assistance here. If you don't have one, use a pill bottle or something similar. Insert the bunch of hair—tips first—then tap the stacker on your tying table so that the tips of the hair become even.

Body in place. Leave lots of room for wing.

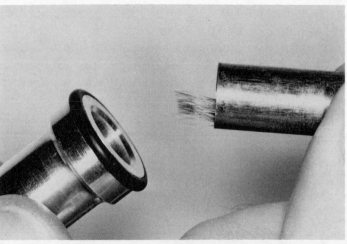

Hair tips made even by use of stacking tool.

6. Carefully remove the stacked hair, keeping the tips even. Position the bunch atop the hook just ahead of the front of the body. The tips should extend well beyond the rear of the hook. The wing is approximately 1½ times the body length.

7. Tie on the bunch using two successive pinches, but don't pinch the material quite as tightly as you would a feather wing. Allow some of the hair to work downward around the shoulders of the fly, but not below the plane of the body. Secure with several tight wraps, directly on top of one another. This will cause the hair to flair, particularly the butt ends in front of the thread.

Positioning the wing. Note that caddisflies have short bodies, relative to wing length.

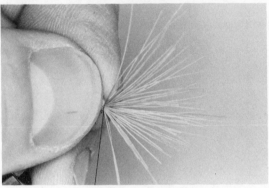

Wing being tied in. Allow butts of hair to flare.

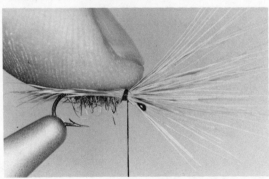

Spread wing to sides a bit with thumb.

Lock butts in flared position with thread.

8. Let the bobbin hang. Then trim the hair into the shape shown in the illustration. This flair of hair represents the caddisflies' legs, aids floatation, and abets twitching.

9. Execute the whip-finish, and apply two coats of cement, letting it soak in well.

Trim butts into shape, as illustrated.

The completed fly, side and top views.

PATTERN DESCRIPTION, FRONT-HACKLE VERSION

This pattern is the same as the no-hackle version, except that a small dry-fly quality hackle is required. It may be brown, grizzly, or cree, or you may use brown and grizzly mixed.

TYING STEPS

1. Tie the fly as described in steps 1–7.
2. After securing the hairwing, trim the butt material as close as you can, then bind down the remainder.
3. Select an undersize hackle, one which would be appropriate for a normal dry fly one hook size smaller. Prepare it, tie it in, and wind it as you would any dry-fly hackle.
4. Whip-finish, and cement. Put a drop of cement at the base of the wings in back of the hackle.

Wing in place for front-hackle version.

The completed front-hackle version.

PATTERN DESCRIPTION—PALMERED VERSION

This pattern is the same as the front-hackle version, except that the hackle is of normal size for the hook being used (size 14 in this case) and long enough to be palmer-wound the length of the body.

TYING STEPS

1. Tie on near the front, wrap to the bend, and tie in the hackle feather.
2. Make the dubbed body.
3. Wind the hackle over the body in evenly spaced, spiraled turns (remember the Wooly Worm?). The number of turns you can obtain depends on the usable length of the feather. Try to make it work out so that your final turn is at the front of the body.
4. Tie off the hackle and create a thread base upon which to mount the wings. Then cut a wide "V" out of the top of the hackle from front to back.
5. Tie on the wing, as you did with the front-hackle version, trimming close and binding down the butts.

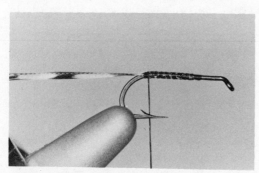

Hackle feather in place for palmered-hackle version.

Palmered hackle being wound.

Top of hackle being trimmed preparatory to mounting of wing.

The completed fly, palmered version.

6. Whip-finish, and cement.

A note about the last version. It is difficult to palmer-hackle a body properly without really good feathers. Obviously, there is the matter of usable length—a short feather probably won't span the length of the body, and you can't tie in a second one in the middle. Of at least equal importance is the matter of conformity. Top-quality hackle tends to have uniform barbule length throughout almost the entire usable portion. This is a very positive attribute, as it gives the fly better balance on the water.

HACKLE-TRIMMING OPTIONS

The silhouette and floatation characteristics of both the front-hackle and palmered-hackle caddis may be varied by some discreet trimming. For a slightly lower, more stable float, trim off the tips of the hackles, about even with the hook point. For an almost-flush float, trim off all of the bottom hackles.

In rough, turbulent water, I leave the hackles untrimmed. For dancing, riffle-type currents, I use the partially trimmed version. The low-floater is often more effective on slower pools. None of this is written in stone—it is a matter of experimenting and discovering what works best in a particular situation.

ABOUT DEER-TYPE HAIRS

You may recall that in the chapter on materials, I described the different properties to look for when selecting hair for dry-fly wings versus clipped bodies or Muddler Minnow heads. The Hairwing Caddis is an exception, because the wing is not your standard upright dry-fly wing. It is what we call a *downwing,* or *tentwing,* and it must contribute substantially to floating the fly, particularly on the hackleless version.

Hair selection for this and most other flies is disciplined by hook size. Quite obviously, one cannot use the coarse, good-floating hair we would choose for a bass bug on a size 20 caddis. Thus, there is a trade off involved—we sacrifice some buoyancy for fineness of texture. The fine type of hair makes neater wings, but doesn't crimp as well. Consequently, I don't tie the hackleless caddis on small hooks, where very fine hair is mandated.

My preferred hairs for the caddis are deer and elk. For spun-and-clipped bodies I also use antelope and caribou. Antelope is very coarse, but is deceptively easy to work with—it flairs beautifully and is a great floater. Caribou is quite fine and soft, which makes it ideal for smaller dry flies.

In the tying instructions I mentioned cleaning out the underfur. This is most critical when using hair for bodies or Muddler heads, because the underfur will tend to bind the hair and prevent it from flairing properly. If you like working with hair and intend to use it extensively, you might consider the purchase of a small fine-tooth comb for cleaning out underfur and short hairs. The tiny steel moustache combs found in specialty shops (Hoffritz, etc.) are perfect for this operation. The small plastic brush/comb instruments women use in working on their eyebrows and lashes are also most serviceable.

20

THE HAIRWING ROYAL COACHMAN

TECHNIQUES TO BE LEARNED

1. The upright/divided hairwing
2. The dry-fly hair tail
3. The Royal Coachman body

This pattern is one of the premier attractor-type dry flies. Reportedly, it was conceived in England during the nineteenth century by a nobleman's coach driver who did double duty as fly-dresser. The original dressing, called just the Coachman, used white quill wings, tied upright and divided. A once-popular American version substituted fan wings made from white duck breast feathers. It was a picturesque fly—but horrible to cast, and without equal as a leader twister.

At some point, the Royal Coachman was crossed with the Wulff series of hairwing flies, which were designed by Lee Wulff for rough-water dry-fly fishing. As a matter of fact, the pattern is also known as the Royal Wulff. The resulting hybrid has become a landmark pattern—perhaps the only one a non-fly-fisherman would recognize.

That this fly works as well as it does is one of the delicious inconsistencies of angling. Realism is definitely not an attribute—don't search the rivers for a Royal Coachman hatch, you might better spend your time looking for a unicorn or the Loch Ness monster. And I wouldn't recommend casting a Hairwing Royal into the sulphur hatch on the Letort, unless you enjoy the sound of laughing trout. But at dusk on a fast riffle, or on off-color water after a spring rain, one can win big with the Royal.

PATTERN DESCRIPTION

HOOK: Dry fly, size 12
THREAD: Black
WINGS: White calf body hair, tail hair, or goat body hair
TAIL: Same as wings
BODY: Peacock herl and red synthetic yarn
HACKLE: Brown, the darker the better

TYING STEPS

1. Tie on near the front and create a thread base for the wings. Because of the complexity of the body on this pattern, the wings must not be positioned too far back, certainly no more than thirty percent of the shank length behind the eye, and perhaps closer to twenty-five percent.

2. Cut off a bunch of hair for the wings. If you are using calf tail, take the shorter hairs near the butt end. In the case of any of the hairs you might use, hold the bunch at approximately a right angle from the skin, so the tips are more or less even, and cut the bunch off at the base, using your coarse-work scissors.

3. Clean out the short hairs and even up the tips in a stacker, as you did with the caddis. Because of its crinkliness, calf tail doesn't respond to stacking all that well. A pinch of unscented talcum powder in the stacker helps, but it's a little messy. I suggest you even up calf tail ends manually.

NOTE: By far the most common mistake made by beginners and experienced tyers alike is using too much hair to make the wings. After removing the short hairs, make an assessment of the remaining bunch and compare it to the illustration.

4. Gauge the length. Hairwings must not be overly long, as this results in a poorly balanced fly. The shank length plus a scant $\frac{1}{16}$ inch (1 mm) will work on a size 12. Adjust for other hook sizes.

5. Position the bunch as prescribed in Step 1 and tie it on with a pinch or two. Don't allow hairs to slip around the sides. A few will do so despite your best efforts, but we will correct that in a moment.

6. Bind down the bunch with a series of tight wraps, working back and forth. Hair requires substantially more binding down than feather fibres, especially calf tail.

7. When satisfied that the wings are secured, pull them upward and force any strays which have slipped down around the shoulders to re-join the bunch.

After cleaning out bunch of hair and running it through the stacker, tie it on as you would a bunch of teal or wood duck. Crimp into upright position.

Lock hair in upright position
with thread.

8. Crimp the hairs into an upright position using the right thumb—and a bit more muscle than you would with feathers. Secure them in position with several tight wraps in front.

9. The wings are divided, crisscrossed, and figure-eighted into position in the same manner as the teal wing on the Foxy Quill, except that a little more thread tension is required. Separate the hairs into two equal bunches with the scissor tips, spread them with your fingers, then do the thread maneuvers as illustrated in the Foxy Quill series.

10. Trim the butts on a slant. Then wrap the thread to the bend, binding them down.

11. Select another small bunch of hair, clean out the short hairs, and tie it on for the tail. Again, be conservative in quantity. The tail should be the same length as the wing.

NOTE: On smaller sizes, or when the fly is intended for use on moderate currents, a hair tail may constitute a bit of overkill. Feel free to substitute a barbule tail, using the same color as the hackle.

Divide and lock in wings, using same
steps as for teal wing on Foxy Quill.

Tail in place.

12. After securing the tail in position, cut it on a counter-taper, so that it and the tapered wing butts complement each other in forming a smooth underbody. Bind them down, wrapping forward and then back to the bend.

13. Tie in a piece of dark brown or black thread. This will be used to reinforce the peacock, as was done on the Brown Hackle.

14. Select four medium-thickness peacock fronds, trim off the first ½ inch or so (13 mm) of the tips, and tie the tip ends in at the base of the tail.

NOTE: The Royal Coachman body is unique. It consists of a bump of peacock, a red band, and then another bump of peacock. Examine all of the tying steps before beginning to construct the body so that you know what's coming, and what the finished product should look like.

15. Make several clockwise twists with the thread-peacock bunch. Then make one turn at the base of the tail.

16. Twist some more, and then make another turn as close as possible to the first one. Two turns should be sufficient.

17. Bind down the herl and thread, working forward with a series of neat, contiguous wraps. You are forming a base for the red band, which is ⅟₁₆ of an inch (2 mm) in length. Do not trim off the peacock and thread.

18. Select a short piece of red synthetic yarn. It need be only long enough for you to hold onto while making two or three turns. The yarn should be very thin, like floss. Reduce it by separating the strands.

NOTE: I favor polypropylene yarn, because it doesn't absorb water and thus retains its color. The original dressing called for red floss, which turned dark burgundy as soon as it got wet and made a negative contribution to floatation.

19. Tie in the yarn, but don't trim off the excess yet.

20. Make two or three turns, forming the band. Tie off with a couple of tight wraps.

21. Bind down both excess tags, working in front of the peacock and thread, which was left hanging. Trim off the yarn.

First bump of peacock.

Red band being wrapped.

Red band in place, excess
being trimmed.

22. Retrieve the peacock and thread, and make another bump in front of the red band, just like the first. Try to allow space for hackle.

23. Bind down the twisted peacock and thread securely along the bottom of the shank. You may wish to wrap the thread under the thorax before trimming, then wrap back to the front of the second bump of herl.

24. Select two brown hackles of appropriate size, tie them in, and hackle the fly, as you did the Foxy Quill. You may use as many turns as space and feathers will allow—this fly should be well hackled.

25. Whip-finish and cement.

Second bump of peacock being secured
by tying down butts in front of
thorax area.

The completed fly.

A few notes about the Hairwing Royal Coachman. The hackle is supposed to be a dark mahogany, which in fly-tying circles is referred to as *Coachman brown*. It does exist, but is not easy to find. Imported hackle seldom runs to that dark a shade, and the domestic growers seem to concentrate on the various shades of duns, creams, gingers, and grizzlies that are in such heavy demand.

Your options are:
- Search around until you find a true Coachman brown cape.
- Settle for medium or fiery brown, which is readily obtainable.
- Purchase a dyed cape.

All of these options are viable. As to the latter, I have seen some really gorgeous dark-brown dye jobs—I own a couple, in fact. Provided the heat of the bath is properly controlled so that feather quality is not affected, a dyed cape is perfectly acceptable.

The Hairwing Royal is often tied in large sizes for use as an Atlantic salmon dry fly or for huge trout. A heavier hook is required, such as a medium-weight wet-fly hook or a Wilson dry-fly salmon hook, which Partridge manufactures. To successfully float such an iron requires lots of good-quality hackle. I often use saddles. While usually more coarse then cape hackles, saddles have the fibre strength necessary to support the additional weight. I may use three or even four feathers to obtain the desired result.

I vividly recall my first experience with salmon dry flies—and not without a degree of pain. I did some professional tying in the early-to-mid-1960s, in a vain effort to make fishing pay for itself. Among my customers were two contractors from around the Albany area—nice guys, and very successful. They had booked a trip to Anticosti Island specifically to fish the dry fly for Atlantic salmon and large brook trout. I dressed them a gross of flies, mostly White Wulffs and Royals, sizes 6 and 8. They were tied on standard dry-fly hooks.

Upon their return, I received a highly animated and explicit phone call from the boys. My flies worked great. The fish loved them—and well they should, for all they had to do to escape was to straighten the bend and spit the fly back at the angler like a dart!

What did I know? I was economically confined to local fishing, where a pound-and-a-half trout might put your picture on the sports page. Years later I chanced onto a pool of enormous brown trout surface feeding on a caddis hatch in a tributary of the Yellowstone. My flies were tied on light-wire dry-fly hooks. I found out first-hand how it feels to experience the dart syndrome.

21

MIXING AND MATCHING

If you have followed the script and can successfully tie the flies in the pattern lessons, you now have a basic arsenal of fourteen assorted patterns, with a few options and variations, right? Wrong! Exactly how many useful patterns you are now equipped to dress is anyone's guess. My estimate would run well into the hundreds.

Does that sound like a big number? Consider that there are at least several dozen variations of soft-hackle patterns alone. Nymph patterns are practically beyond count—and so are streamers. The Wooly Worm and Wooly Bugger are tied in a wide range of colors and sizes. Winged wet flies and emergers are numerous. Add to these the many classic and contemporary dry flies now within your realm of capability and my estimate becomes quite realistic.

True, there are flies you aren't prepared to tie, at least not from just the training contained in this volume. One of the attributes of a good beginner's book on any subject is that it doesn't attempt to cover too much. Another attribute is that what *is* covered is taught in depth and in accordance with the best methodology known to the writer.

Let's examine what is meant by mixing and matching as it relates to fly patterns. The dressing for the Quill Gordon, a historic dry fly, is as follows:

HOOK: Dry fly, size 12 or 14

THREAD: Black, brown, or olive

WINGS: Barred wood-duck flank, upright and divided

TAIL: Medium dun hackle barbules

BODY: Stripped quill from eyed section of a peacock tail feather

HACKLE: Medium dun

You can tie this pattern merely by substituting dun hackle and tail and wood duck wing, and by following the instructions for the Foxy Quill.

Replace the peacock quill body with a stripped quill from a dark ginger or medium brown feather and you have Art Flick's marvelous Red Quill. Substitute a dubbed body of appropriate color and you have a Hendrickson. Make the dubbed body, tail, and hackle of a cream or straw-cream shade, and you have a Light Cahill. Make the dubbed body grey and the tail and hackle dark ginger or medium brown, and you have a Dark Cahill.

Are you beginning to get the idea?

Remember the Blue-Winged Olive? Change the body color to grey and you have dressed a Blue Dun. Substitute a quill body, and you have the Blue Quill. Make the wings, tail, and hackle light-grey and the body creamy-orangish, and the Pale Evening Dun is created. Incidentally, the Blue-Winged Olive is effective with an olive-colored quill body. Use a magic marker or dyed quill.

Want to tie a Cahill Quill? Simply tie a Foxy Quill with wood-duck wings and cream or straw-cream tail and hackle. How about a Ginger Quill? All you do is substitute a grey hackle-tip wing and ginger tail and hackle.

Having learned the Hairwing Royal Coachman, you can tie the entire Wulff series of dry flies—White, Grey, Brown, or whatever. Having learned the Dun Variant, you can tie the other variants in Art Flick's book. You can tie the March Brown and the Grey Fox. In fact, you can tie many more dry-fly patterns than is practical to carry astream at a given time. You will end up rotating fly boxes, as I do.

As to wet flies, the underwater world is your oyster. As I mentioned, a veritable host of soft-hackle flies can be created by mixing, matching, and substituting various body materials and colors, ribbings, and hackles. The simple nymph we tied can be used to simulate many mayfly nymphs merely via color, texture, and size alterations. It serves as a stonefly nymph, too.

Remember the turkey-quill wing option we learned in the March Brown wet-fly lesson? That very technique will enable you to tie the murderous Hare's Ear and Leadwing Coachman wet flies, simply by using slate-color duck or goose wing feathers for the wing sections and appropriate body and tail material. Mastery of the brown mallard flank wing from that same lesson equips the tyer to dress all of the popular wood-duck flank-wing patterns.

And then there are streamers, an enormous and diverse field of fly-tying unto itself. Some patterns use rather esoteric materials and techniques that weren't within the scope of the *Primer,* but there are literally dozens of great patterns which call for wings of hair, feather, or marabou—all three of which you know. The bodies are commonly made of combinations of floss, tinsel, wool, herl, and dubbing, which is also in your bag.

Structurally, there is virtually no difference between the Mickey Finn and the Black-Nosed Dace, another of Art Flick's legendary creations. Nor is there any technical difference between the marabou-wing version of the Golden Darter and the Black Ghost Marabou, a great favorite of mine. Being capable of tying the feather wing opens up a vast array of patterns, including the classic designs of Lew Oatman, Carrie Stevens, and others.

You may not be ready for full-dressed Atlantic salmon flies, but there is nothing to prevent you from dressing the simple and intermediate-level hairwing patterns. These are nothing more than a marriage of the streamer and the wet fly. Except for certain patterns which call for complex body construction because of the corresponding full-dress version, I can't think of any hairwing salmon fly you couldn't tie, based on what you've learned from the *Primer.* And believe me, hairwings are the answer in salmon fishing. Full-dress patterns are for framing.

This could become a very long chapter. I could touch upon many subtle innovations which alter patterns—all of which you are equipped to utilize. I could talk about new and evolving materials, such as Flashabou, a synthetic streamer-wing material that has revolutionized Pacific salmon fly design. I could describe structural variations of the dry fly, such as parachute hackle and the thorax style. But I'm going to save that and more, hopefully for another book.

There is something else you now have the ability to do, something which is most important and terrifically rewarding: you can make up your own fly patterns and innovations. If you think it is thrilling to take a fish on a fly you've tied yourself (and it is!), wait until you have a two-dozen-trout evening on a pattern of your own design! This is as close to experiencing what an artist must feel as this artisan will ever come. To tie what one sees—not only with one's eyes but with one's spirit—adds a universal dimension to fly-tying.

You are a fly-tyer now. Congratulations, and welcome to the club.